Connected Mathematics 2™

Additional Practice and Skills Workbook

Grade 6

Glenda Lappan
James T. Fey
William M. Fitzgerald
Susan Friel
Elizabeth Difanis Phillips

PEARSON
Prentice
Hall

Boston, Massachusetts
Upper Saddle River, New Jersey

Connected Mathematics™ Project was developed at Michigan State University with financial support from the Michigan State University Office of the Provost, Computing and Technology, and the College of Natural Science.

Connected Mathematics™ is based upon work supported by the National Science Foundation under Grant No. MDR 9150217 and Grant No. ESI 9986372. Opinions expressed are those of the authors and not necessarily those of the Foundation.

The Michigan State University authors and administration have agreed that all MSU royalties arising from this publication will be devoted to purposes supported by the Department of Mathematics and the MSU Mathematics Enrichment Fund.

Acknowledgments The people who made up the *Connected Mathematics 2* team—representing editorial, editorial services, design services, and production services—are listed below. Bold type denotes core team members.

Leora Adler, Judith Buice, Kerry Cashman, Patrick Culleton, Sheila DeFazio, Katie Hallahan, Richard Heater, **Barbara Holllingdale, Jayne Holman,** Karen Holtzman, **Etta Jacobs,** Christine Lee, Carolyn Lock, Catherine Maglio, **Dotti Marshall,** Rich McMahon, Eve Melnechuk, Terri Mitchell, **Marsha Novak,** Irene Rubin, Donna Russo, Robin Samper, Siri Schwartzman, **Nancy Smith,** Emily Soltanoff, **Mark Tricca,** Paula Vergith, Roberta Warshaw, Helen Young.

ISBN 0-13-165613-9

30 29 28 27   V001   18 17 16 15

Table of Contents

Additional Practice

1. For each of the following, use the set of clues to determine the secret number.

  a. Clue 1   The number has two digits.

     Clue 2   The number has 13 as a factor.

     Clue 3   The sum of the digits of the number is 11.

  b. Clue 1   The number is prime.

     Clue 2   The number is less than 19.

     Clue 3   The sum of the digits of the number is greater than 7.

2. The numbers 10, 20, and 30 on the 30-board in the Factor Game all have 10 as a factor. Does *any* number that has 10 as a factor also have 5 as a factor? Explain your reasoning.

3. The numbers 14, 28, and 42 on the 49-board in the Factor Game all have 7 as a factor and also have 2 as a factor. Does *any* number that has 7 as a factor also have 2 as a factor? Explain your reasoning.

4. Look carefully at the numbers 1–30 on the 30-board used for playing the Factor Game. Pick the two different numbers on the 30-board that will give you the largest number when you multiply them together, and then answer the following questions.

  a. What two numbers did you pick? What is the product of the two numbers?

  b. Explain why the product of the two numbers you chose is the largest product you can get using two different numbers from the 30-board.

  c. List all the proper factors of the product. Explain how you found the factors.

Additional Practice (continued)

5. For each of the following, find three different numbers that can be multiplied together so that the given number is the product. Do not use 1 as one of the numbers.

    a. 150   **b.** 1,000   **c.** 24   **d.** 66

6. The number sequence 4, 6, 10 is a multiple of the number sequence 2, 3, 5 because the sequence 4, 6, 10 can be found by multiplying all the numbers in the sequence 2, 3, 5 by 2. That is, $4 = 2 \times 2, 6 = 2 \times 3, 10 = 2 \times 5$.

    a. The number sequence 15, 25, 10 is a multiple of what number sequence?

    b. Find two different sequences that are multiples of the number sequence 1, 4, 7.

    c. Given a number sequence, how many different sets of multiples of that sequence do you think there are? Explain your reasoning.

7. Given the following sets of numbers, write as many different multiplication and division statements as you can. For example, if the numbers are 5, 7, 35, you can write:

    $5 \times 7 = 35$ $7 \times 5 = 35$ $35 \div 5 = 7$ $35 \div 7 = 5$

    a. 6, 4, 24   **b.** 96, 12, 8, 3, 32   **c.** 6, 27, 108, 12, 4, 18, 9

    d. When is a number called a factor of a number? A divisor of a number?

Skill: Factors, Multiples, and Primes

List all the factors of each number.

1. 12

2. 45

3. 41

4. 54

5. 48

6. 100

7. 117

Skill: Factors, Multiples, and Primes (continued)

Tell whether the second number is a multiple of the first.

8. 2; 71   **9.** 1; 18   **10.** 3; 81   **11.** 4; 74

12. 9; 522   **13.** 8; 508   **14.** 13; 179   **15.** 17; 3,587

Tell whether each number is prime or composite.

16. 53   **17.** 86   **18.** 95   **19.** 17

20. 24   **21.** 27   **22.** 31   **23.** 51

24. 103   **25.** 47   **26.** 93   **27.** 56

28. Make a list of all the prime numbers from 50 through 75.

Additional Practice

1. Alicia has made a rectangle using 24 square tiles. If she adds the length and width of her rectangle together, she gets 11. What is the length and width of Alicia's rectangle? Explain your reasoning.

2. Jennifer has made a rectangle using 48 square tiles. If she adds the length and width of her rectangle together she gets a prime number. What is the length and width of Jennifer's rectangle? Explain your reasoning.

3. List all of the factor pairs for each of the following numbers.
   a. 56   **b.** 42   **c.** 31   **d.** 80   **e.** 75   **f.** 108   **g.** 225

4. Phillip is thinking of a number that is less than 20 and has three factor pairs. Phillip also says that if he adds together the factors in the factor pairs he gets 19, 11, and 9. What is Phillip's number? Explain how you found your answer.

Additional Practice *(continued)*

5. In each of the rectangles shown below, only the tiles along the length and width are shown. For each rectangle, explain how many square tiles it would take to make each rectangle.

a. 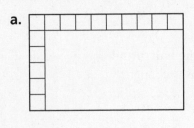   b. 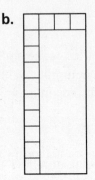   c.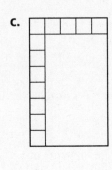

6. a. Draw and label a Venn diagram in which one circle represents the factors of 12 and another circle represents the factors of 13. Place the numbers from 1 to 15 in the appropriate regions of the diagram.

   b. What do you notice about the numbers in the intersection? Why does this happen?

   c. What is another set of labels, one for each of the two circles, that gives the same numbers in the intersection as you found in part (b)? Explain your reasoning.

7. a. Draw and label a Venn diagram in which one circle represents the multiples of 5 and another circle represents the multiples of 2. Place the numbers from 1 to 40 in the appropriate regions of the diagram.

   b. What do you notice about the numbers in the intersection? Why does this happen?

   c. Where would you place 75 in the diagram? Where would you place 90? Explain your reasoning.

8. Karl added four numbers together and got an even sum. Three of the numbers are 42, 35, and 77. What can you say about the fourth number? Explain your reasoning.

Additional Practice

1. On Saturdays, the #14 bus makes roundtrips between Susan's school and the mall, and the #11 bus makes roundtrips between the mall and the museum. Next Saturday, Susan wants to take the bus from her school to the museum. A #14 bus leaves Susan's school every 15 minutes, beginning at 7 A.M. It takes the bus 30 minutes to travel between the school and the mall. A #11 bus leaves the mall every 12 minutes, beginning at 7 A.M.

   a. If Susan gets on the #14 at 9:30 A.M., how long will she have to wait at the mall for a #11 bus? Explain your reasoning.

   b. If Susan gets on the #11 bus at the museum and arrives at the mall at 11:48 A.M., how long will she have to wait for the #14 bus? Explain your reasoning.

   c. At what times between 9 A.M. and noon are the #14 and #11 buses at the mall at the same time? Explain your reasoning.

2. Kyong has built two rectangles. Each has a width of 7 tiles.

   a. If each rectangle is made with an even number of tiles that is greater than 40 but less than 60, how many tiles does it take to make each rectangle? Explain your reasoning.

   b. What is the length of each of Kyong's rectangles? Explain your reasoning.

   c. Without changing the number of tiles used to make either rectangle, Kyong rearranges the tiles of each rectangle into different rectangles. What is a possibility for the length and width of each of Kyong's new rectangles? Explain your reasoning.

Additional Practice *(continued)*

3. Jack plays on a basketball team after school (or on the weekend) every third day of the month. He babysits his younger brother after school every seventh day of the month. How many times during a 30-day month, if any, will Jack have a conflict between basketball and babysitting? Explain your reasoning.

4. Suppose you have two different numbers which are both prime.
   a. What is the least common multiple of the numbers? Explain your reasoning.

   b. What is the greatest common factor? Explain your reasoning.

5. Find the least common multiple and the greatest common factor for each pair of numbers:
   a. 8 and 12 **b.** 7 and 15 **c.** 11 and 17 **d.** 36 and 108

   e. For which pairs in parts (a)–(d) is the least common multiple the product of the two numbers? Why is this so? What is special about the numbers in these pairs?

6. Find the greatest common factor of each pair of numbers:
   a. 4 and 12 **b.** 5 and 15 **c.** 10 and 40 **d.** 25 and 75

   e. When is the greatest common factor of two numbers one of the two numbers? Explain your reasoning.

Skill: Least Common Multiple

List multiples to find the LCM of each set of numbers.

1. 5, 10

2. 2, 3

3. 6, 8

4. 4, 6

5. 8, 10

6. 5, 6

7. 12, 15

8. 8, 12

9. 9, 15

10. 6, 15

11. 6, 9

12. 6, 18

13. 3, 5

14. 4, 5

15. 9, 21

16. 7, 28

17. One radio station broadcasts a weather forecast every 18 minutes and another station broadcasts a commercial every 15 minutes. If the stations broadcast both a weather forecast and a commercial at noon, when is the next time that both will be broadcast at the same time?

Skill: Greatest Common Factor

List the factors to find the GCF of each set of numbers.

1. 8, 12

2. 18, 27

3. 15, 23

4. 17, 34

5. 24, 12

6. 18, 24

7. 5, 25

8. 20, 25

9. 10, 15

10. 25, 75

11. 14, 21

12. 18, 57

13. 32, 24, 40

14. 25, 60, 75

15. 12, 35, 15

16. 15, 35, 20

17. Cameron is making bead necklaces. He has 90 green beads and 108 blue beads. What is the greatest number of identical necklaces he can make if he wants to use all of the beads?

Additional Practice

1. Find the prime factorization for each of the numbers below.

   a. 630   **b.** 144   **c.** 1,011   **d.** 133   **e.** 23

2. Solve each of the multiplication mazes given below. Record your solution for each maze by copying the maze on your paper and then tracing out the path through the maze.

a.

Maze 924

Enter →

2	3	7	2
6	2	7	11
5	4	9	10

Exit →

b.

Maze 1080

2	8	6	3
27	5	7	2
2	5	2	9

Exit →

Enter →

c.

Maze 38220

Enter →

14	39	70	91
7	2	20	60
42	15	2	2
98	26	13	7

Exit →

d.

Maze 210

Enter →

3	10	3	14
2	3	5	7
35	2	105	2
7	15	6	3

Exit →

Additional Practice (continued)

3. For each of the pairs of numbers given below, find the greatest common factor and the least common multiple.

   a. 25 and 105   **b.** 27 and 81   **c.** 36 and 63

4. An odd number that is less than 160 has exactly three different prime factors. What is the number? Explain your reasoning.

5. What number has the prime factorization $2^3 \times 3^2 \times 5^2$?

6. a. Name a pair of numbers whose greatest common factor is the same as one of the numbers.

   b. Name another pair of numbers whose greatest common factor is the same as one of the numbers.

   c. Make a conjecture about what must be true about the least common multiple of any number pairs in which one number is the greatest common factor of the other number.

7. a. Are 45 and 64 relatively prime? Explain your reasoning.

   b. Are 25 and 36 relatively prime? Explain your reasoning.

   c. Is it possible for two numbers that are both even to be relatively prime? Why or why not?

   d. How can you choose one number so that it will be relatively prime to any other number?

Skill: Prime Factorization

Complete each factor tree.

1.

2.

3.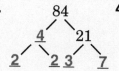

4.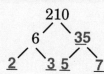

Find the prime factorization of each number.

5. 58

6. 72

7. 40

8. 310

Find the number with the given prime factorization.

9. $2 \times 2 \times 5 \times 7 \times 11$

10. $7 \times 11 \times 13 \times 17$

11. There are 32 students in a class. How many ways can the class be divided into groups with equal numbers of students? What are they?

Write the prime factorization. Use exponents where possible.

12. 78

13. 126

14. 125

15. 90

16. 92

17. 180

Skill: Prime Factorization *(continued)*

Use prime factorization to find the LCM of each set of numbers.

18. 18, 21   **19.** 15, 21   **20.** 18, 24   **21.** 21, 24

22. At a store, hot dogs come in packages of eight and hot dog buns come in packages of twelve. What is the least number of packages of each type that you can buy and have no hot dogs or buns left over?

Use factor trees to find the GCF of each set of numbers.

23. 57, 27   **24.** 24, 48   **25.** 56, 35   **26.** 29, 87

27. The GCF of two numbers is 850. Neither number is divisible by the other. What is the smallest that these two numbers could be?

Additional Practice

1. Find all of the numbers less than 1,000 that have 3 as their only prime factor. Explain your strategy for finding all of these numbers.

2. A *number sequence* is an ordered series of numbers that follow a pattern or rule. Jason has developed a secret rule for generating his own number sequence. Here are the first five terms in the sequence: 3, 15, 45, 225, 675, ... and so on. Use Jason's sequence to answer the following questions.

   a. What is Jason's rule for finding the numbers in his number sequence? Explain how you found your answer.

   b. What are the next two terms in Jason's number sequence?

   c. What is the greatest common factor of all the terms in Jason's sequence, no matter how many new numbers he adds to the sequence? Explain your reasoning.

3. In the 1,000-locker problem, which students touched the lockers indicated?

   a. both lockers 13 and 19

   b. lockers 12, 16, and 20

4. In the 1,000-locker problem, what was the last locker touched by the students indicated?

   a. both students 20 and 25

   b. both students 13 and 19

   c. all three students 3, 4, and 5

   d. all three students 30, 40, and 50

5. A set of consecutive numbers that contains no prime numbers is called a *prime desert*. For example, the set {14, 15, 16} is a prime desert because it is a set of consecutive numbers and none of the numbers are prime. Find the prime desert that has the most numbers in it where all the numbers are less than 50.

6. For each of the sets of clues below, find the secret number.

   a. Clue 1   The number is less than 130.

   Clue 2   The number ends in a 5.

   Clue 3   The number is a multiple of a prime that is greater than 20, but less than 30.

   b. Clue 1   The number ends in a 0.

   Clue 2   The number is a multiple of 21.

   Clue 3   The number is less than 400.

7. Find the prime factorization of each of the following numbers.

   a. 190   **b.** 319   **c.** 255   **d.** 406

Additional Practice

1. a. For each of the fraction strips below, write a fraction that expresses how much of the strip is shaded.

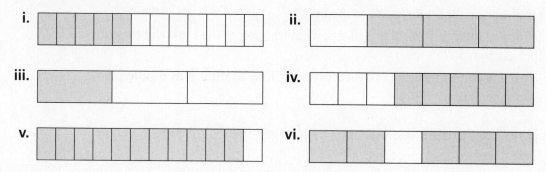

b. For each of the six fraction strips above, write a fraction that expresses how much of the strip is not shaded.

c. What is the relationship between the fraction you wrote for the shaded part and the fraction you wrote for the unshaded part for each of the six fraction strips? Explain your reasoning.

2. The drawing shows the controls on a small, portable stereo system. Use the drawing to answer each of the following questions. Record all of your answers as fractions.

a. What fraction of the total volume is the stereo playing?

b. What fraction of the total bass output is the stereo playing?

c. What fraction of the total treble output is the stereo playing?

d. If the volume of the stereo is turned down to half the current volume, what fraction of the total volume will be the new volume? Explain your reasoning.

e. If the bass control on the stereo is adjusted up so that the stereo is playing at double the bass output it is playing at now, what fraction of the total bass output will be the new bass output? Explain your reasoning.

3. A bag contains 24 marbles (**Note:** You may want to use 24 cubes, chips, marbles, or other objects to help you solve this problem.)

a. If 16 of the marbles are removed from the bag to play a game, what fraction of the marbles are left in the bag?

b. Of the 16 marbles taken from the bag, one-fourth are put back in the bag. Now how many marbles are in the bag? Explain your reasoning.

Additional Practice (continued)

4. Joey's father stops at the gas station to buy gas. The car has a 16-gallon tank, and the fuel gauge says there is $\frac{3}{8}$ of a tank of gas.

   a. How many gallons of gas are in the tank?

   b. If Joey's father buys 6 gallons of gas, what fraction of the tank will the car's fuel gauge read?

   c. What fraction of the gas tank is empty after Joey's father puts 6 gallons of gas in the tank?

5. For parts (a)–(b), use fraction strips or some other method to name the point with a fraction.

   a.

   b.

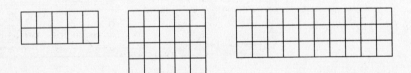

6. For parts (a)–(c), copy the grids on your paper. Shade each grid to represent the given fraction.

   a. Represent the fraction $\frac{4}{5}$ on each grid.

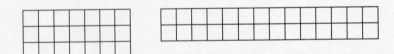

   b. Represent the fraction $\frac{3}{7}$ on each grid.

   c. Represent the fraction $\frac{1}{6}$ on each grid.

7. Tony is driving from Alma, Michigan to Elizabeth City, North Carolina. The drive covers a total distance of 1,100 miles. Tony's car can travel 400 miles on a full tank of gas. How many tanks of gas will Tony's car need for the entire trip? Explain your reasoning.

Additional Practice

1. For each pair of fractions, insert a less-than symbol ($<$), greater-than symbol ($>$), or an equals symbol ($=$) between the fractions to make the true statement.

   a. $\frac{1}{2}$ $\frac{5}{10}$ **b.** $\frac{1}{3}$ $\frac{2}{5}$ **c.** $\frac{5}{12}$ $\frac{1}{3}$

   d. $\frac{4}{5}$ $\frac{2}{3}$ **e.** $\frac{3}{4}$ $\frac{8}{10}$ **f.** $\frac{5}{8}$ $\frac{3}{7}$

2. **a.** For each pair of fractions, insert a less-than symbol ($<$), greater-than symbol ($>$), or an equals symbol ($=$) between the fractions to make the true statement.

   i. $\frac{2}{3}$ $\frac{2}{5}$ **ii.** $\frac{4}{6}$ $\frac{4}{5}$ **iii.** $\frac{3}{4}$ $\frac{3}{8}$

   b. Describe a way to compare two fractions when the numerators are the same.

3. **a.** For each pair of fractions, insert a less-than symbol ($<$), greater-than symbol ($>$), or an equals symbol ($=$) between the fractions to make the true statement.

   i. $\frac{2}{5}$ $\frac{4}{5}$ **ii.** $\frac{4}{9}$ $\frac{7}{9}$ **iii.** $\frac{5}{11}$ $\frac{3}{11}$

   b. Describe a way to compare two fractions when the denominators are the same.

4. For each group of fractions, rewrite the fractions in order from least to greatest.

   a. $\frac{2}{3}, \frac{1}{2}, \frac{3}{4}, \frac{2}{6}$ **b.** $\frac{24}{4}, \frac{1}{4}, \frac{11}{16}, \frac{1}{7}$

   c. $\frac{1}{2}, \frac{1}{5}, \frac{1}{3}, \frac{1}{9}, \frac{1}{6}$ **d.** $\frac{11}{16}, \frac{3}{4}, \frac{3}{8}, \frac{1}{2}, \frac{3}{16}$

5. For each of the six fraction strips below, write *two* fractions that express the portion of the strip that is shaded.

   a.    **b.**

   c. 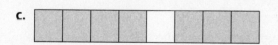   **d.**

   e.    **f.**

6. Find a fraction between each pair of fractions given.

   a. $\frac{4}{7}$ and $\frac{5}{7}$ **b.** $\frac{1}{3}$ and $\frac{1}{4}$ **c.** $\frac{1}{8}$ and $\frac{2}{8}$

Additional Practice (continued)

7. Copy each number line below and estimate where the number 1 would be. Explain the strategy you used for each number line.

a.

b.

c.

8. For each shape below, write a fraction to express the portion of the entire shape that is shaded.

a.   b.   c. 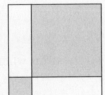 d.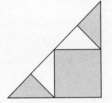

9. Copy and complete the following table:

Fraction	$\frac{7}{4}$	▓	$\frac{35}{3}$	$\frac{19}{4}$	▓	▓
Mixed Number	▓	$3\frac{2}{3}$	▓	▓	$2\frac{5}{6}$	$7\frac{1}{2}$

10. Lisa has two oranges that are the same size but each one is divided differently. One orange has been divided into five equal-size sections and the other orange has been divided into ten equal-size sections.

   a. If Brian eats three pieces of the orange with five sections, what fraction of the orange will he get?

   b. Lisa gave John the orange with ten sections. John wants to eat the same amount as Brian. How many pieces of his orange will John have to eat? Explain.

   c. Lisa bought a new orange that she wants to share equally among three people. This orange has been divided into five equal-size sections. Explain how Lisa should cut the orange so three people can share it.

Skill: Comparing Fractions

Name the fractions modeled and determine if they are equivalent.

1. ▭ 2. ▭ 3. ▭

Compare each pair of fractions. Use <, >, or =.

4. $\frac{7}{8}$ ▢ $\frac{3}{10}$ 5. $\frac{4}{5}$ ▢ $\frac{1}{2}$ 6. $\frac{6}{12}$ ▢ $\frac{4}{8}$ 7. $\frac{7}{15}$ ▢ $\frac{11}{15}$

8. $\frac{4}{5}$ ▢ $\frac{6}{10}$ 9. $\frac{7}{12}$ ▢ $\frac{2}{3}$ 10. $\frac{8}{15}$ ▢ $\frac{1}{2}$ 11. $\frac{10}{15}$ ▢ $\frac{8}{12}$

12. $\frac{4}{9}$ ▢ $\frac{7}{9}$ 13. $\frac{2}{5}$ ▢ $\frac{3}{8}$ 14. $\frac{1}{2}$ ▢ $\frac{11}{20}$ 15. $\frac{7}{16}$ ▢ $\frac{1}{2}$

Order from least to greatest.

16. $\frac{1}{4}, \frac{1}{3}, \frac{1}{6}$ 17. $\frac{1}{2}, \frac{5}{6}, \frac{7}{8}$ 18. $\frac{1}{4}, \frac{2}{5}, \frac{3}{8}$

19. $\frac{7}{8}, \frac{5}{9}, \frac{2}{3}$ 20. $\frac{3}{8}, \frac{5}{6}, \frac{1}{2}$ 21. $\frac{9}{10}, \frac{11}{12}, \frac{15}{16}$

22. $\frac{3}{4}, \frac{1}{2}, \frac{7}{8}$ 23. $\frac{5}{9}, \frac{2}{3}, \frac{7}{12}$ 24. $\frac{15}{16}, \frac{7}{8}, \frac{1}{2}$

25. A pattern requires a seam of at least $\frac{5}{8}$ in. Rachel sewed a seem $\frac{1}{2}$ in. wide.
    Did she sew the seam wide enough? Explain.

Skill: Mixed Numbers and Improper Fractions

Write each mixed number as an improper fraction.

1. $1\frac{7}{8}$

2. $2\frac{3}{4}$

3. $7\frac{1}{3}$

4. $8\frac{2}{3}$

5. $3\frac{3}{4}$

6. $4\frac{1}{4}$

7. $5\frac{5}{6}$

8. $1\frac{9}{10}$

9. $3\frac{11}{12}$

10. $4\frac{7}{8}$

11. $2\frac{3}{5}$

12. $2\frac{7}{15}$

Write each improper fraction as a mixed number in simplest form.

13. $\frac{15}{2}$

14. $\frac{8}{3}$

15. $\frac{5}{2}$

16. $\frac{7}{3}$

17. $\frac{11}{10}$

18. $\frac{7}{6}$

19. $\frac{9}{8}$

20. $\frac{20}{8}$

21. $\frac{27}{12}$

22. $\frac{26}{18}$

23. $\frac{35}{21}$

24. $\frac{17}{4}$

25. Find the improper fraction with a denominator of 6 that is equivalent to $5\frac{1}{2}$.

26. Find the improper fraction with a denominator of 12 that is equivalent to $10\frac{1}{4}$.

Additional Practice

1. In the diagram, the hundredths grid is the whole. Use the grid to answer each of the following questions and write each answer in both decimal and fraction form.

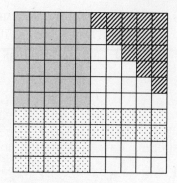

   a. What portion of the grid is shaded gray?

   b. What portion of the grid is striped?

   c. What portion of the grid is checkered?

   d. What portion of the grid is blank?

2. For each pair of numbers, insert a less-than symbol (<), a greater-than symbol (>), or an equals symbol (=) between the numbers to make a true statement.

   a. 0.305   0.35   **b.** 0.123   0.1002

   c. 0.25   0.25000   **d.** 0.25   0.025

   e. 3.45   3.045   **f.** 12.03   12.30

3. For each pair of numbers, insert a less-than symbol (<), greater-than symbol (>), or an equals symbol (=) between the numbers to make a true statement.

   a. 2.5 $2\frac{2}{5}$ **b.** 0.65 $\frac{2}{3}$ **c.** 0.8 $\frac{4}{7}$

   d. $\frac{5}{8}$ 0.625   **e.** 0.3 $\frac{3}{7}$ **f.** 2.1 $1\frac{9}{10}$

   g. $\frac{11}{12}$ $\frac{11}{11}$ **h.** $\frac{3}{6}$ 0.5   **i.** 9 $8\frac{8}{10}$

4. Copy each number line below. In each case, two of the marks are labeled. Label the unlabeled marks with decimal numbers.

   a.

   0.3   0.6

   b.

   0.11   0.13

   c.

   0.03   0.12

   d.

                              0.5   0.75

Additional Practice (continued)

5. Name three fractions that are equivalent to each decimal below. Explain your reasoning. Draw a picture if it helps you explain your thinking.

   a. 0.60   **b.** 1.7   **c.** 0.05   **d.** 2.3   **e.** 0.15   **f.** 0.625

6. Name a decimal that is equivalent to each fraction below. Explain your reasoning. Draw a picture if it helps you explain your thinking.

   a. $\frac{1}{2}$ **b.** $\frac{3}{15}$ **c.** $\frac{7}{4}$ **d.** $\frac{3}{8}$ **e.** $\frac{111}{20}$ **f.** $\frac{18}{24}$

7. Sarah can jog at a steady pace of 4.75 miles per hour, and Tony can jog at a steady pace of 4.25 miles per hour.

   a. How many miles can Sarah jog in 30 minutes? Explain your reasoning.

   b. How many miles can Tony jog in 30 minutes?

   c. If Sarah and Tony jog for 45 minutes, how much farther will Sarah go than Tony? Explain your reasoning.

8. Each small square on the grid represents $\frac{1}{5}$.

   a. What whole number is represented by the whole grid?

   b. What decimal is represented by the shaded region of the grid?

9. Each small square on the grid represents 0.25.

   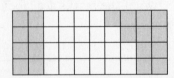

   a. What whole number is represented by the whole grid?

   b. What fraction is represented by the shaded region of the grid?

10. Paul claims that the fraction $\frac{1}{3}$ is a good estimate for the decimal 0.3.

    a. Do you agree or disagree with Paul's claim? Explain your reasoning.

    b. Is Paul's estimate less than, greater than, or equal to 0.3? Explain your reasoning.

Skill: Fractions and Decimals

Write the decimal represented by each model as a fraction.

1.    **2.** 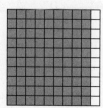   **3.**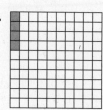

Write each decimal as a fraction.

4. 0.6   **5.** 1.25   **6.** 0.74   **7.** 0.29

8. 0.635   **9.** 0.8   **10.** 0.95   **11.** 0.645

Write each fraction as a decimal.

12. $\frac{9}{100}$ **13.** $\frac{7}{25}$ **14.** $\frac{3}{50}$ **15.** $\frac{1}{125}$

Write each of the decimal numbers in words.

16. 12.873

17. 8.0552

18. 0.00065

Skill: Comparing and Ordering Decimals

Insert <, >, or = in each box to make a true statement.

1. 0.62 ☐ 0.618   **2.** 9.8 ☐ 9.80   **3.** 1.006 ☐ 1.02   **4.** 41.3 ☐ 41.03

5. 2.01 ☐ 2.011   **6.** 1.400 ☐ 1.40   **7.** 5.079 ☐ 5.08   **8.** 12.96 ☐ 12.967

9. 15.8 ☐ 15.800   **10.** 7.98 ☐ 7.89   **11.** 8.02 ☐ 8.020   **12.** 5.693 ☐ 5.299

Order each set of decimals on a number line.

13. 0.2, 0.6, 0.5

14. 0.26, 0.3, 0.5, 0.59, 0.7

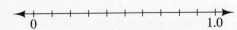

15. Three points are graphed on the number line below. Write statements comparing 0.3 to 0.5 and 0.5 to 0.7.

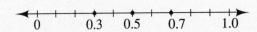

16. Models for three decimals are shown below.

    a. Write decimal names that each shaded part represents.

    b. Rewrite the decimals in order from least to greatest.

Additional Practice

1. For each of the grids given below, express the shaded region of the grid as a fraction, a decimal, and a percent.

a. 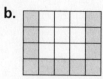   b. 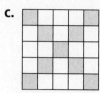   c.

d.   e.   f.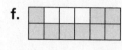

2. Angie and Jim conducted a survey of their sixth-grade classmates in their mathematics class. They found out the following information:

- 70% of the students in the class do homework three or more nights each week.

- Of the students who do homework three or more nights each week, half do homework five nights each week.

a. What percentage of the students in the class do homework two nights or less each week? Explain your reasoning.

b. What fraction of the students in the class do homework five nights each week? Explain your reasoning.

c. What percentage of students in the class do homework three or four nights a week? Explain your reasoning.

d. From the information provided, can you tell how many students are in the class? Explain why or why not.

3. In a class of 24 sixth-graders, 25% walk to school, $\frac{1}{8}$ ride bicycles to school, $\frac{1}{3}$ take the bus to school, and the remainder of the class are driven to school by their parents or guardians.

a. How many students in the class walk to school? Explain your reasoning.

b. How many students in the class ride bicycles to school? Explain your reasoning.

c. How many students in the class take the bus to school?

d. What fraction of the class are driven to school by their parent or guardian? Explain your reasoning.

e. What percentage of the students in the class walk, ride bicycles or the bus, or are driven to at school by a parent or guardian? Explain your reasoning.

Additional Practice (continued)

4. Express the shaded region of each drawing as a fraction, a decimal, and as a percent.

a.
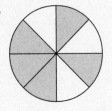

b.
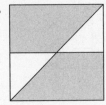

c.
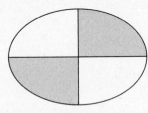

d.
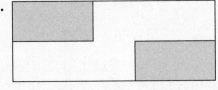

5. In one competition, the archery team had to shoot at targets from three different distances: 10 m, 20 m, and 30 m. The number of hits and the number of shots for each distance are given below. Write their score for each round as a fraction, a decimal, and a percent.

a. at 10 m: 42 hits out of 50 shots

b. at 20 m: 37 hits out of 50 shots

c. at 30 m: 18 hits out of 50 shots

6. Fill in the missing parts of the table.

Fraction	Decimal	Percent
$\frac{3}{8}$		
	0.88	
		35%
$1\frac{1}{4}$		
	0.625	
		275%

Skill: Percents

Shade each grid to represent each of the following percents.

1. 53%

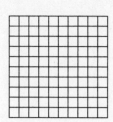

2. 23%

3. 71%

Write a percent for each shaded figure.

4.

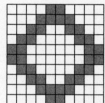

5.

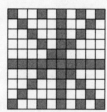

6.

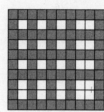

The table shows the fraction of students who participated in extracurricular activities from 1965 to 2000. For Exercises 7–14, complete the table by writing each fraction as a percent.

Students' Extracurricular Choices

Year	1965	1970	1975	1980	1985	1990	1995	2000
Student participation (fraction)	$\frac{3}{4}$	$\frac{8}{10}$	$\frac{17}{20}$	$\frac{39}{50}$	$\frac{21}{25}$	$\frac{19}{25}$	$\frac{87}{100}$	$\frac{9}{10}$
Student participation (percent)	**7.**	**8.**	**9.**	**10.**	**11.**	**12.**	**13.**	**14.**

Write each fraction as a percent.

15. $\frac{4}{5}$

16. $\frac{3}{5}$

17. $\frac{9}{10}$

18. $\frac{3}{10}$

19. $\frac{6}{25}$

20. $\frac{7}{100}$

21. $\frac{9}{50}$

22. $\frac{9}{25}$

23. $\frac{2}{5}$

24. $\frac{7}{10}$

25. $\frac{4}{25}$

26. $\frac{16}{25}$

Skill: Percents, Fractions, and Decimals

Write each percent as a decimal and as a fraction.

1. 46%   **2.** 17%   **3.** 90%   **4.** 5%

Write each decimal as a percent and as a fraction.

5. 0.02   **6.** 0.45   **7.** 0.4   **8.** 0.92

Write each fraction as a decimal and as a percent.

9. $\frac{3}{5}$ **10.** $\frac{7}{10}$ **11.** $\frac{13}{25}$ **12.** $\frac{17}{20}$

13. Write each fraction or decimal as a percent. Write the percent (without the percent sign) in the puzzle.

ACROSS	DOWN
1. $\frac{3}{5}$	**1.** $\frac{13}{20}$
2. $\frac{1}{5}$	**2.** 0.25
3. 0.55	**3.** $\frac{1}{2}$
5. 0.23	**4.** $\frac{3}{20}$
6. $\frac{7}{20}$	**5.** 0.24
7. 0.17	**6.** $\frac{3}{10}$
9. 0.4	**7.** 0.1
10. $\frac{9}{25}$	**8.** $\frac{4}{25}$

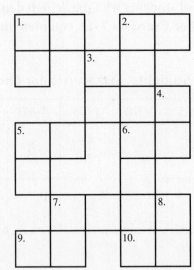

Additional Practice

Answer parts (a) and (b) for each polygon shown in Exercises 1–6.

   a. Is the shape a regular polygon? Explain why or why not.

   b. Could the shape be used to tile a surface? Make a sketch to demonstrate
     your answer.

1.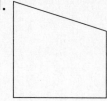

2.

3.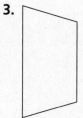

4.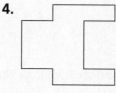

5.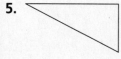

6.

Additional Practice (continued)

7. The shape below is composed of four polygons.

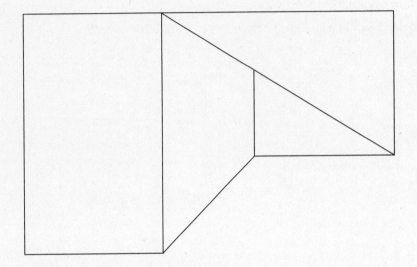

a. Describe the four polygons in the shape.

b. Can the shape be used to tile a surface? Make a sketch to demonstrate your answer.

Skill: Polygons

Name each polygon according to the number of sides.

1.

2.

3.

4.

5.

6.

Use the diagram below to identify all the polygons for each name.

7. quadrilateral

8. parallelogram

9. rhombus

10. rectangle

11. square

12. trapezoid

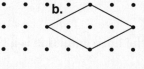

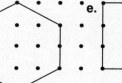

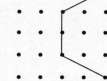
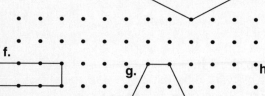
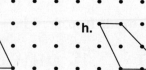

Skill: Line Symmetry

Tell whether each figure has line symmetry. If it does, draw the line(s) of symmetry. If not, write *none*.

1.

2.

3.

4.

5.

6.

Draw the missing half of each figure so that the vertical line is a line of symmetry.

7.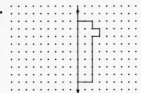

8.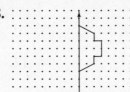

9.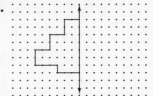

Draw the missing half of each figure so that the horizontal line is a line of symmetry.

10.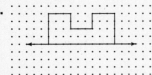

11.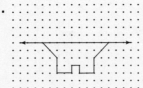

12.

Is there a line of symmetry for each word? If so, draw it.

13. B O X

14. T O O T

15. C H I C O

16. M O M

Additional Practice

1. Use the circular grid below to answer the following questions.

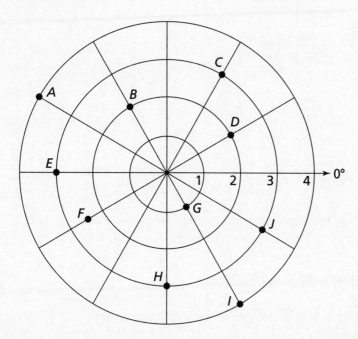

a. Find the (distance, angle measure) coordinates for points *A* through *J*.

b. What is the distance from point *A* to point *J*? Explain how you found your answer.

c. What is the distance from point *F* to point *D*?

d. What is the distance from point *B* to point *I*?

e. What is the measure of the angle with vertex at the origin and sides that pass through points *H* and *J*? Explain how you found your answer.

f. What is the measure of the angle with vertex at the origin and sides that pass through points *A* and *I*?

Additional Practice *(continued)*

2. Use the diagram of the polygon shown below to answer the following questions.

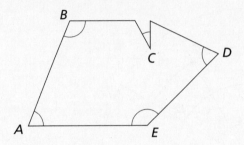

    a. Estimate the measures of angles *A* through *E*.

    b. Use your angle ruler to find the measure of each angle. How do the measures compare with your estimates from part (a)?

    c. Is the polygon a regular polygon? Why or why not?

3. Use the diagram below and what you know about angle relationships to answer the following questions.

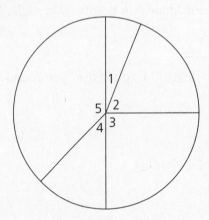

    a. What is the measure of angle 3?

    b. The measure of angle 1 is one-fourth of the measure of angle 3. What is the measure of angle 1?

    c. What is the measure of angle 2?

    d. The measure of angle 4 is twice the measure of angle 1. What is the measure of angle 4?

    e. What is the measure of angle 5?

Name _____ Date _____ Class _____

Skill: Angles

Measure each angle with an angle ruler.

1.

2.

3.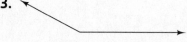

4.

Draw an angle for each measure.

5. 88°

6. 66°

7. For the polygon below, measure the angles with an angle ruler.

Skill: Angles and Parallel Lines

In each diagram below, lines L_1 and L_2 are parallel lines cut by a transversal. Find the measure of each numbered angle.

1.

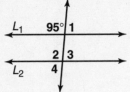

2.

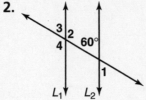

3.

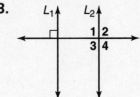

4. Use the figure below. Is line L_1 parallel to line L_2? Explain how you could use an angle ruler to support your conjecture.

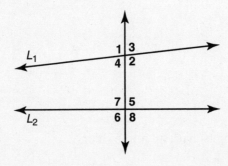

Additional Practice

1. An isosceles triangle has two 50° angles. What is the measure of the third angle? Explain how you found your answer.

2. One angle of an isosceles triangle measures 100°. What are the measures of the other two angles? Explain your reasoning.

3. Two of the angles of a parallelogram each measure 75°. What are the measures of the other two angles? Explain your reasoning.

4. One angle of a parallelogram measures 40° and another angle measures 140°. What are the measures of the other two angles? Explain how you found your answer.

5. Can a parallelogram have two 45° angles and two 75° angles? Why or why not?

6. For each of the shapes below, find the unknown angle measure without using your angle ruler.

a.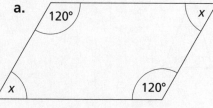

b.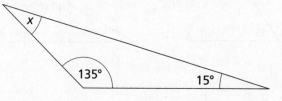

c.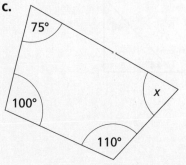

d.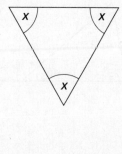

Skill: Angle Sums and Exterior Angles of Polygons

Find the measure of each angle labeled x.

1.
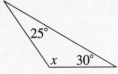
25°
x   30°

2.

51°
62°   x

3.

23°
x   121°

4.
74°
x   53°

5.
x
54°   54°

6.
50°   x
80°

Find the measure of each angle labeled x.

7.
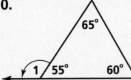
71°   48°
108°   x

8.
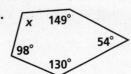
x   149°
98°   54°
130°

9.
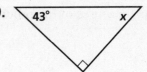
43°   x

Find the measure of angle 1 in each figure.

10.
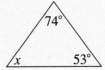
65°
1   55°   60°

11.
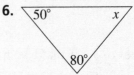
1
111°
30°   39°

12.

1
37°
75° 68°

13.
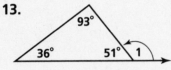
93°
36°   51°   1

14.
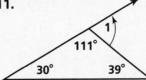
61°
79°   40°   1

15.

46°
1   44°

Additional Practice

1. A quadrilateral has two sides of length 6. The sum of the lengths of the other two sides is 15. Use this information to answer the following questions.

   a. Suppose the two sides of length 6 are right next to each other. What might the lengths of the other two sides be? Explain your reasoning.

   b. Suppose the quadrilateral is a rectangle and the two sides of length 6 are opposite each other. What would the lengths of the other two sides have to be? Explain how you found your answer.

   c. Could the quadrilateral have two sides of length 6, one side of length 13.5, and one side of length 1.5? Explain why or why not.

2. Bob has sketched an equilateral triangle. The sum of the lengths of the sides is 12. What is the length of each side of Bob's triangle? Explain your reasoning.

3. Angela has sketched a rectangle. She says that the lengths of the sides of the rectangle add to 26, and the length of one side is 7. What are the length and width of Angela's rectangle? Explain how you found your answer.

4. Use the triangle to answer the following questions.

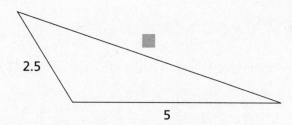

2.5

5

   a. Alex estimates that the unknown side length is about 4.5. How do you think Alex's estimate compares with the actual length? Explain your reasoning.

   b. Jennifer estimates that the unknown side length is about 8. How do you think Jennifer's estimate compares with the actual length? Explain.

   c. Use what you have learned about making triangles with polystrips to estimate the length of the unknown side. Explain why you think your estimate is close to the actual length.

Additional Practice *(continued)*

5. The figure below is made up of squares and triangles. Use the design below and what you know about angle relationships to answer the following questions.

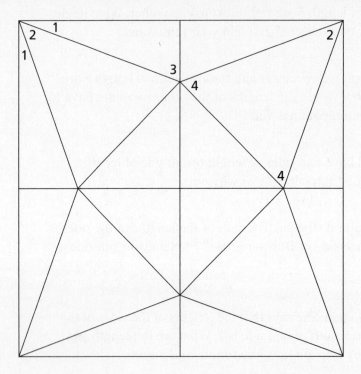

a. If the measure of angle 1 is 25°, what is the measure of angle 2? Explain your reasoning.

b. If the measure of angle 1 is 25°, what is the measure of angle 3? Explain your reasoning.

c. If the measure of angle 1 is 25°, what is the measure of angle 4? Explain your reasoning.

Additional Practice

1. Suppose you roll a red number cube and a green number cube and form a fraction with the number on the red number cube as the numerator and the number on the green number cube as the denominator.

   a. List all the possible fractions.

   b. List all the fractions that are between $\frac{2}{3}$ and $1\frac{1}{2}$.

   c. List all the fractions that are between $2\frac{1}{3}$ and $3\frac{2}{3}$.

2. For each part, state whether the sum of the fractions is less than, greater than, or equal to 1. Explain your thinking.

   a. $\frac{3}{8} + \frac{2}{5}$

   b. $\frac{5}{10} + \frac{3}{4}$

   c. $\frac{3}{12} + \frac{3}{6}$

   d. $\frac{1}{2} + \frac{4}{8}$

   e. $\frac{4}{7} + \frac{7}{12}$

   f. $\frac{4}{3} + \frac{1}{100}$

   g. $\frac{1}{4} + \frac{2}{3}$

   h. $\frac{9}{20} + \frac{5}{11}$

   i. $\frac{9}{12} + \frac{2}{8}$

Additional Practice (continued)

3. "Close to One" is a game that uses the "Getting Close" game cards that show fractions less than 1. The object of "Close to One" is to estimate a sum of two fractions that is as close to 1 as possible without exceeding 1. On each turn, the player draws one card. This is the starting value. Then, the player draws three more cards and chooses the one that will make the sum as close to 1 as possible without exceeding 1.

In each sample turn below, the starting value is followed by the value of three game cards. Choose the fraction that will make the sum as close to 1 as possible without exceeding 1. Explain the reasoning for your choice.

   a. $\frac{1}{3}$ $\frac{1}{8}, \frac{1}{4}, \frac{1}{2}$

   b. $\frac{3}{4}$ $\frac{1}{8}, \frac{1}{3}, \frac{1}{2}$

   c. $\frac{2}{5}$ $\frac{1}{4}, \frac{1}{2}, \frac{3}{4}$

   d. $\frac{9}{10}$ $\frac{7}{10}, \frac{3}{4}, \frac{2}{3}$

   e. $\frac{1}{10}$ $\frac{1}{8}, \frac{1}{5}, \frac{1}{4}$

   f. $\frac{3}{8}$ $\frac{4}{9}, \frac{5}{6}, \frac{9}{10}$

4. For each set of fractions, list all the possible pairs whose sum is between 1 and $1\frac{1}{2}$. Explain your thinking.

   a. $\frac{1}{2}, \frac{3}{4}, \frac{7}{8}$

   b. $\frac{1}{3}, \frac{9}{10}, \frac{6}{5}$

   c. $\frac{3}{4}, \frac{7}{8}, \frac{9}{10}$

   d. $\frac{1}{4}, \frac{1}{2}, \frac{3}{5}$

   e. $\frac{1}{10}, \frac{2}{3}, \frac{5}{4}$

   f. $\frac{1}{2}, \frac{3}{5}, \frac{7}{10}$

5. Rosa and Tony need to estimate how much it will cost to purchase the following supplies for their class project.

   4 pieces of posterboard at $2.89 each

   1 bottle of glue at $1.19

   2 booklets of construction paper at $4.99 each

   2 pairs of scissors at $0.59 each

   a. Estimate the cost of the supplies that Rosa and Tony need to buy.

   b. In this situation, would it be better to overestimate or underestimate? Explain.

Skill: Estimating With Fractions

Write the fraction shown by each model. Then determine whether the number is closest to $0, \frac{1}{2},$ or 1.

1.

2.

Estimate each sum. Use the benchmarks $0, \frac{1}{2},$ and 1.

3. $\frac{5}{16} + \frac{5}{8}$

4. $\frac{10}{12} + \frac{4}{5}$

5. $\frac{1}{10} + \frac{1}{2}$

6. $\frac{3}{4} + \frac{3}{8}$

7. $\frac{1}{12} + \frac{6}{11}$

8. $\frac{8}{14} + \frac{4}{7}$

9. $\frac{1}{6} + \frac{5}{8}$

10. $\frac{1}{10} + \frac{5}{6}$

11. $\frac{9}{10} + \frac{7}{8}$

12. $\frac{1}{12} + \frac{9}{10}$

13. $\frac{15}{16} + \frac{11}{12}$

14. $\frac{1}{8} + \frac{9}{10}$

15. Name three fractions whose benchmark is $\frac{1}{2}$.

16. Name three fractions whose benchmark is 1.

Skill: Estimating With Mixed Numbers

Estimate each sum.

1. $2\frac{1}{6} + 7\frac{1}{9}$ **2.** $4\frac{7}{8} + 8\frac{1}{5}$ **3.** $2\frac{7}{9} + 4\frac{1}{8}$ **4.** $14\frac{3}{4} + 9\frac{7}{8}$

5. $6\frac{7}{8} + \frac{11}{12}$ **6.** $1\frac{1}{8} + 1\frac{1}{5}$ **7.** $2\frac{1}{6} + 1\frac{9}{10}$ **8.** $4\frac{9}{10} + 4\frac{7}{8}$

9. $5\frac{6}{7} + \frac{2}{3}$ **10.** $\frac{1}{7} + 2\frac{7}{8}$ **11.** $2\frac{4}{5} + 1\frac{5}{8}$ **12.** $\frac{2}{13} + 3\frac{1}{18}$

13. $42\frac{1}{6} + 6\frac{1}{16}$ **14.** $6\frac{2}{15} + 1\frac{3}{4}$ **15.** $19\frac{5}{6} + 20\frac{1}{12}$ **16.** $2\frac{1}{4} + 3\frac{15}{16}$

17. $\frac{2}{9} + 2\frac{7}{8}$ **18.** $7\frac{1}{8} + 2\frac{3}{11}$ **19.** $3\frac{4}{5} + 2\frac{1}{8}$ **20.** $\frac{3}{5} + \frac{7}{8}$

21. Julia bought stock at $28\frac{1}{8}$ per share. The value of each share increased by $6\frac{5}{8}$. How much is each share of stock now worth?

Additional Practice

1. Jack and Helen are making cookies. The recipe says to combine $\frac{1}{2}$ cup of butter with $\frac{3}{4}$ cup chocolate chips and $\frac{3}{8}$ cup chopped nuts.

   a. When these three ingredients are mixed together, how many cups of the mixture will Jake and Helen have? Show your work.

   b. Jack and Helen decide to triple the recipe.
      i. How many cups of butter will be needed?

      ii. How many cups of chocolate chips will be needed?

      iii. How many cups of chopped nuts will be needed?

   c. When the ingredients for the tripled recipe are combined, how many cups of the mixture will Jack and Helen have?

2. Mr. Larson is planning the seating for a school recital. He needs to reserve $\frac{1}{3}$ of the seats for students and $\frac{1}{6}$ of the seats for parents.

   a. After reserving seats for students and parents, what fraction of the seats in the auditorium are left?

   b. Mr. Larson's principal tells him that he also needs to reserve $\frac{1}{8}$ of the seats for teachers and school officials. The remainder can be used for open seating. What fraction of the seats are now left for open seating?

   c. Later, Mr. Larson's principal says he should reserve $\frac{1}{4}$ of the seats for students from other middle schools. Are there enough seats left? If not, explain why not; otherwise, state what fraction of the seats will be available for open seating.

Additional Practice (continued)

3. Find the value of N that makes each number sentence correct.

   a. $\frac{3}{4} + N = \frac{19}{20}$ **b.** $N - \frac{1}{2} = \frac{3}{8}$ **c.** $\frac{1}{6} + \frac{5}{12} = N$

   d. $N - \frac{1}{5} = \frac{7}{20}$ **e.** $\frac{7}{9} - \frac{2}{3} = N$ **f.** $\frac{3}{2} + N = \frac{9}{4}$

   g. $\frac{4}{5} + \frac{1}{6} = N$ **h.** $\frac{1}{2} - N = \frac{1}{5}$ **i.** $\frac{3}{7} + \frac{4}{21} = N$

4. The shaded region represents one whole unit.

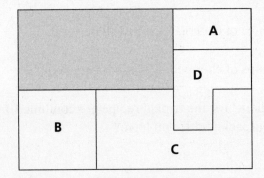

   a. What fraction of the whole is each of the other four regions A, B, C, D?

   b. Based on your answers to part (a), find the area of each of the following:

   i. region A + region B   **ii.** region C + region D

   iii. region B − region D   **iv.** region C − region A

   c. If the entire outer rectangle is considered the whole, what fraction of the whole would the shaded gray area be? Explain your reasoning.

5. Find each sum. Describe any patterns you see.

   a. $\frac{1}{2} + \frac{1}{3}$ **b.** $\frac{1}{3} + \frac{1}{4}$ **c.** $\frac{1}{4} + \frac{1}{5}$

   d. $\frac{1}{5} + \frac{1}{6}$ **e.** $\frac{1}{6} + \frac{1}{7}$ **f.** $\frac{1}{7} + \frac{1}{8}$

Skill: Adding and Subtracting Fractions

Find each sum or difference.

1. $\frac{1}{4} + \frac{2}{4}$

2. $\frac{7}{10} - \frac{4}{10}$

3. $\frac{5}{8} - \frac{3}{8}$

4. $\frac{1}{8} + \frac{5}{8}$

5. $\frac{5}{8} + \frac{2}{8}$

6. $\frac{3}{10} + \frac{6}{10}$

7. $\frac{2}{5} - \frac{1}{10}$

8. $\frac{5}{8} - \frac{1}{4}$

9. $\frac{3}{10} + \frac{4}{5}$

10. $\frac{11}{16} + \frac{5}{8}$

11. $\frac{2}{3} - \frac{1}{6}$

12. $\frac{3}{5} + \frac{7}{10}$

13. What is the total amount of sugar in the recipe at the right?

Martha's Cookie Recipe
1 cup shortening
2 eggs
$\frac{1}{4}$ cup white sugar
$\frac{1}{4}$ cup brown sugar
$1\frac{1}{2}$ cups flour
1 teaspoon vanilla

14. Martha decides to double the recipe. How much brown sugar will she use?

15. At the tea shop, $\frac{5}{15}$ of the customers purchased green tea, $\frac{2}{15}$ of the customers purchased jasmine tea, and $\frac{5}{15}$ of the customers purchased herbal tea. What portion of the customers purchased another type of tea?

16. A piece of fabric is $\frac{7}{9}$ yard long. A piece of ribbon is $\frac{2}{9}$ yard long. How many more yards of ribbon do you need to have equal lengths of fabric and ribbon?

Skill: Adding and Subtracting Mixed Numbers

Find each sum or difference.

1. $4\frac{3}{10} + 5\frac{2}{5}$

2. $3\frac{7}{8} + 2\frac{1}{2}$

3. $5\frac{2}{3} + 3\frac{1}{4}$

4. $6\frac{3}{4} + 2\frac{1}{2}$

5. $1\frac{1}{12} + 3\frac{1}{6}$

6. $9\frac{2}{5} + 10\frac{3}{10}$

7. $7\frac{1}{3} + 5\frac{11}{12}$

8. $11\frac{7}{10} + 4$

9. $2\frac{2}{3} + 4\frac{3}{4}$

10. $10\frac{11}{16} - 3\frac{7}{8}$

11. $8\frac{1}{3} - 2\frac{3}{8}$

12. $9 - 3\frac{2}{5}$

13. $5\frac{3}{16} - 2\frac{3}{8}$

14. $8\frac{1}{6} - 3\frac{2}{5}$

15. $7\frac{1}{2} - 3$

16. $2\frac{3}{4} - 1\frac{1}{8}$

17. $4\frac{1}{8} - 2\frac{1}{16}$

18. $9\frac{2}{3} - 3\frac{5}{6}$

19. Sam grew three pumpkins for the pumpkin growing contest. The pumpkins weighed $24\frac{1}{8}$ pounds, $18\frac{2}{4}$ pounds, and $32\frac{5}{16}$ pounds. Find the combined total weight of Sam's pumpkins.

20. Robbie needs to buy fencing for his square vegetable garden that measures $16\frac{3}{4}$ feet on a side. One side borders the back of the garage. The fencing costs $4 per feet. Estimate how much the fencing will cost.

Additional Practice

1. Find each product. Show your work.

   a. $\frac{2}{3} \times \frac{1}{2}$ **b.** $\frac{3}{5} \times \frac{10}{9}$ **c.** $\frac{3}{4} \times \frac{8}{9}$

   d. $\frac{3}{2} \times \frac{5}{6}$ **e.** $\frac{2}{7} \times \frac{1}{3}$ **f.** $\frac{3}{8} \times \frac{12}{15}$

   g. $\frac{9}{10} \times \frac{1}{6}$ **h.** $\frac{1}{2} \times \frac{6}{7}$ **i.** $360 \times \frac{7}{9}$

2. In a recent survey of 440 people, $\frac{1}{4}$ said that they watched television every evening, $\frac{2}{5}$ said they watched five or six nights each week, and the remainder said they watched four nights a week or less.

   a. How many people in the survey watched television every evening? Explain how you found your answer.

   b. How many people surveyed watched television five or six nights each week?

   c. What fraction of the people surveyed watched television four nights each week or less? Explain how you found your answer.

   d. How many people surveyed watch television four nights each week or less?

3. Jack and Phil are selling advertisements for the yearbook. A full-page ad will cost $240. Advertisers who want only a fraction of a page will be charged that fraction of $240. Jack and Phil's layout for one page is shown at the right.

   a. What fraction of the whole page does each of the six regions occupy?

   b. How much should Jack and Phil charge an advertiser who wants to place an ad that fills area A? Explain how you found your answer.

   c. How much should Jack and Phil charge an advertiser who wants to place an ad that fills area D?

   d. How much should an ad that fills area F cost?

   e. Jack and Phil have sold advertising space in areas B, E, and C.

      i. How much did they collect for the three ads?

      ii. What fraction of the page is left for other advertisers?

Additional Practice (continued)

4. A recipe for granola cookies calls for $\frac{1}{2}$ cup of butter and $\frac{1}{4}$ cup of chopped nuts. Because Jane likes moist cookies without too many nuts, she decides to increase the amount of butter by half and decrease the amount of chopped nuts by half.

   a. How much butter is required for Jane's new recipe? Explain how you got your answer.

   b. What amount of chopped nuts is required for Jane's new recipe? Explain your reasoning.

   c. Since Jane increased the butter by half and decreased the nuts by half, is the combined amount of butter and nuts the same as in the original recipe? Explain why or why not.

5. Paul has $\frac{3}{5}$ of a roll of speaker wire left. His sister uses $\frac{1}{4}$ of it to set up speakers in her room.

   a. How much of the whole roll of speaker wire did Paul's sister use?

   b. What fraction of the whole roll is left? Explain your answer.

6. For each set of multiplication problems, determine whether the products are equal or whether one product is greater. Describe any patterns you see.

   a. $\frac{1}{3} \times \frac{2}{5}$ and $\frac{2}{3} \times \frac{1}{5}$

   b. $\frac{7}{8} \times \frac{6}{5}$ and $\frac{6}{8} \times \frac{7}{5}$

   c. $\frac{3}{10} \times \frac{5}{9}$ and $\frac{5}{10} \times \frac{3}{9}$

   d. $\frac{3}{7} \times \frac{5}{8}$ and $\frac{5}{7} \times \frac{3}{8}$

7. If each person in North America throws away $3\frac{2}{3}$ pounds of garbage each day, how many pounds of garbage does each person throw away in a year?

Skill: Multiplying Fractions

Draw a model to find each product.

1. $\frac{1}{6} \times \frac{3}{4}$

2. $\frac{2}{5} \times \frac{1}{2}$

Find each product.

3. $\frac{3}{5}$ of 10

4. $\frac{1}{4}$ of 12

5. $\frac{2}{3}$ of 6

6. $\frac{4}{5}$ of $\frac{5}{8}$

7. $\frac{5}{6}$ of $\frac{3}{8}$

8. $\frac{3}{5}$ of $\frac{1}{2}$

9. $\frac{3}{4}$ of 12

10. $\frac{2}{5}$ of 15

11. $\frac{3}{5}$ of $\frac{3}{4}$

12. $\frac{1}{2} \times \frac{1}{3}$

13. $\frac{1}{8} \times \frac{3}{4}$

14. $\frac{2}{5} \times \frac{7}{11}$

15. $\frac{2}{3}$ of $\frac{1}{4}$

16. $\frac{2}{5} \times \frac{1}{2}$

17. $\frac{1}{4}$ of $\frac{4}{5}$

18. $\frac{5}{6} \times \frac{2}{5}$

19. A kitten eats $\frac{1}{4}$ cup of cat food. Another cat in the same household eats 6 times as much. How much food does the cat eat?

Skill: Multiplying Mixed Numbers

Find each product.

1. $2\frac{5}{6} \times 1\frac{3}{4}$

2. $3\frac{3}{8} \times 7\frac{1}{4}$

3. $5\frac{3}{8} \times 2\frac{7}{8}$

4. $\frac{1}{4} \times 5\frac{2}{5}$

5. $1\frac{1}{2} \times 5\frac{1}{3}$

6. $\frac{3}{4} \times 1\frac{3}{5}$

7. $3\frac{1}{3} \times 3\frac{3}{10}$

8. $5\frac{1}{2} \times \frac{2}{5}$

9. $1\frac{2}{3} \times 3\frac{3}{4}$

10. Ken used all of a piece of lumber to build a bookshelf. If he made three shelves that are each $2\frac{1}{2}$ feet long, how long was the piece of lumber?

11. Deanna's cake recipe needs to be doubled for a party. How much of each ingredient should Deanna use?

Cake Recipe		
ingredient	*amount*	*doubled amount*
flour	$2\frac{1}{4}$ cups	
sugar	$1\frac{3}{4}$ cups	
butter	$1\frac{1}{2}$ cups	
milk	$\frac{3}{4}$ cup	

Additional Practice

1. Find each quotient. Describe any patterns you see.

   a. $20 \div 2$ **b.** $20 \div 1$ **c.** $20 \div \frac{1}{2}$ **d.** $20 \div \frac{1}{4}$ **e.** $20 \div \frac{1}{8}$

2. LiAnn works in the Olde Tyme Soda Shoppe. The shop sells milkshakes, double milkshakes, and triple milkshakes. A shake uses $\frac{1}{8}$ cup of syrup, a double shake uses $\frac{1}{4}$ cup of syrup, and a triple shake uses $\frac{3}{8}$ cup of syrup. How many shakes of each kind could she make with 3 cups of syrup?

3. Three groups of students are sharing leftover pizza (all the same size originally). In which group does each student get the most pizza? Explain your choice.

   A. Six students equally share $\frac{3}{4}$ of a pizza.

   B. Three students equally share $\frac{1}{3}$ of a pizza.

   C. Four students equally share $\frac{2}{3}$ of a pizza.

4. Find each quotient.

   a. $12 \div \frac{1}{2}$ **b.** $12 \div \frac{1}{3}$ **c.** $3 \div \frac{2}{3}$

   d. $\frac{7}{8} \div 4$ **e.** $1\frac{2}{3} \div 6$ **f.** $\frac{5}{6} \div \frac{1}{3}$

   g. $1\frac{1}{4} \div 2\frac{1}{2}$ **h.** $\frac{8}{5} \div \frac{3}{10}$ **i.** $1\frac{1}{2} \div \frac{3}{4}$

Additional Practice (continued)

5. Max noticed a pattern in some fraction division problems that he computed.

$$\frac{6}{8} \div \frac{3}{8} \text{ gives the same answer as } 6 \div 3.$$

$$\frac{7}{10} \div \frac{3}{10} \text{ gives the same answer as } 7 \div 3.$$

$$\frac{9}{5} \div \frac{2}{5} \text{ gives the same answer as } 9 \div 2.$$

$$\frac{4}{7} \div \frac{5}{7} \text{ gives the same answer as } 4 \div 5.$$

Describe the pattern that Max found. Explain why it works.

6. Sam, Trish, and Shanti are making signs for the spring dance. Sam can make a sign in $\frac{3}{4}$ of an hour, Trish can make a sign in $\frac{2}{3}$ of an hour, and Shanti can make a sign in $\frac{3}{5}$ of an hour.

   a. How many complete signs can each person make in 4 hours?

   b. Who has the most time left over after finishing their last complete sign? How do you know?

7. How many bows can you make from 5 meters of ribbon if making a bow takes $\frac{1}{4}$ of a meter of ribbon?

Skill: Dividing Fractions

1. Draw a diagram to show how many $\frac{3}{4}$-foot pieces of string can be cut from a piece of string $4\frac{1}{2}$ feet long.

Find each quotient.

2. $\frac{1}{12} \div \frac{5}{6}$

3. $4 \div \frac{1}{3}$

4. $6 \div \frac{3}{4}$

5. $5 \div \frac{9}{10}$

6. $8 \div \frac{2}{3}$

7. $\frac{4}{5} \div 2$

8. $\frac{7}{8} \div 3$

9. $\frac{5}{6} \div 5$

10. $\frac{4}{9} \div 8$

11. $\frac{3}{4} \div \frac{1}{4}$

12. $\frac{7}{8} \div \frac{1}{4}$

13. $\frac{5}{6} \div \frac{1}{12}$

14. How many $\frac{3}{4}$-cup servings are there in a 6-cup package of rice?

15. Study the tangram pieces at the right. If the entire square is 1, find the fractional value of each piece. You can copy the tangram and cut the pieces to compare them.

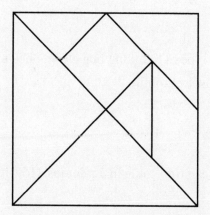

Skill: Dividing Mixed Numbers

Find each quotient.

1. $1\frac{1}{2} \div \frac{2}{3}$

2. $1\frac{1}{2} \div \frac{3}{2}$

3. $\frac{3}{4} \div 1\frac{1}{3}$

4. $2\frac{1}{2} \div 1\frac{1}{4}$

5. $2\frac{1}{2} \div 2\frac{1}{4}$

6. $1\frac{3}{4} \div \frac{3}{4}$

7. $1\frac{7}{10} \div \frac{1}{2}$

8. $3\frac{1}{4} \div 1\frac{1}{3}$

9. $4\frac{1}{2} \div 2\frac{1}{2}$

10. $6 \div 3\frac{4}{5}$

11. $4\frac{3}{4} \div \frac{7}{8}$

12. $5\frac{5}{6} \div 1\frac{1}{3}$

13. Rosa makes $2\frac{1}{2}$ cups of pudding. How many $\frac{1}{3}$-cup servings can she get from the pudding?

14. One type of lightning bug glows once every $1\frac{1}{2}$ seconds. How many times can it glow in 1 minute?

15. Bea can run $\frac{1}{6}$ mile in 2 minutes. How long should it take her to run 2 miles?

Additional Practice

1. Find the area and the perimeter of each of the four shapes below.

a.

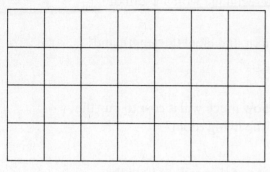

b.

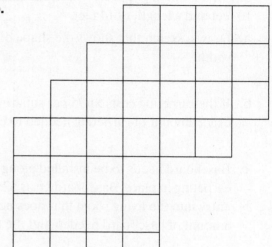

c.

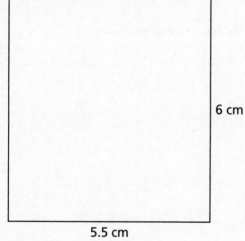

6 cm

5.5 cm

d.

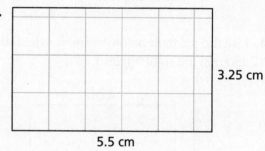

3.25 cm

5.5 cm

Additional Practice *(continued)*

2. Susan is helping her father measure the living room floor because they want to buy new carpeting. The floor is in the shape of a rectangle with a width of 10 feet and a length of 14 feet.

   a. Draw a sketch that shows the shape of the floor and label the length and width.

   b. If the carpeting costs $1.75 per square foot, how much will it cost to buy the exact amount of carpeting needed to carpet the living room?

   c. Baseboard needs to be installed along the base of the walls to hold the carpeting in place. Baseboard costs $2.35 per foot. There is one 6-foot wide entry into the living room that does not need baseboard. Find the exact amount of baseboard needed and the exact cost.

3. Ellen drew a rectangle. She says the area of her rectangle is 7 square units and the perimeter is 16 units. Could Ellen be correct about the perimeter and area of her rectangle? Explain.

4. Use the diagram below to answer the following questions. (All angles in the diagram are right angles.)

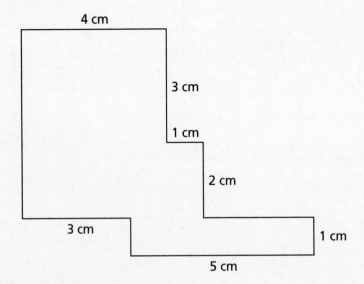

   a. What is the perimeter of the figure?

   b. What is the area of the figure?

   c. Explain how you found your answers for parts (a) and (b).

Additional Practice (continued)

5. Find the area and perimeter of each figure below.

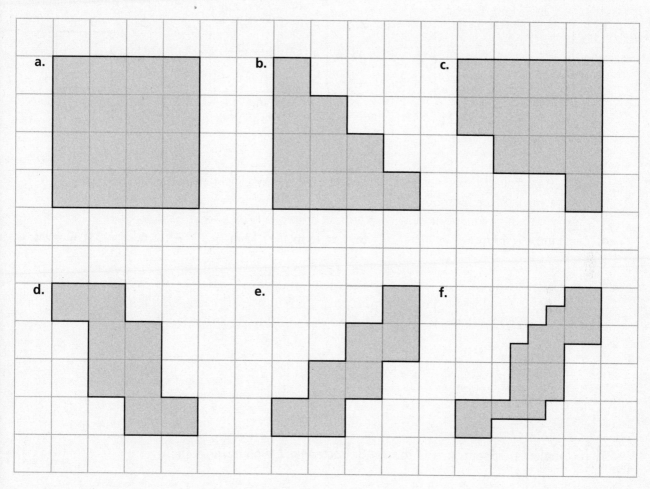

a.   b.   c.

d.   e.   f.

6. Find the area and perimeter of each of the following rectangles.

Rectangle	Area	Perimeter
a. 3 in. ⬚ 7 in.		
b. ⬚ 3.5 in. 3.5 in.		
c. Length: 25 cm; width: 8 cm		
d. Length: 6.7 cm; width: 4.9 cm		

Skill: Area and Perimeter of Rectangles

Find the perimeter and area of each rectangle.

1.

8 cm

15 cm

2.

12 in.

20 in.

3. 6 cm

6 cm

4. $\ell = 5$ in., $w = 13$ in.

5. $\ell = 18$ m, $w = 12$ m

6. $\ell = 3$ ft, $w = 8$ ft

7. rectangle: $l = 16$ mm, $w = 12$ mm

8. rectangle: $l = 65$ mi, $w = 48$ mi

9. The length of a rectangle is 8 centimeters. The width is 6 centimeters.

   a. What is the area?

   b. What is the perimeter?

10. The area of a rectangle is 45 square inches.
One dimension is 5 inches. What is the perimeter?

Skill: Area and Perimeter of Rectangles (continued)

Find the area of each figure.

11. 4 m

4 m

12. 23 cm

5 cm

13.

19 yd

23 yd   30 yd

37 yd

14.

12 cm

3 cm

9 cm   4 cm   2 cm

7cm

15. The figure at the right contains only squares.
Each side of the shaded square is 1 unit.
What is the length, width, and area of the figure?

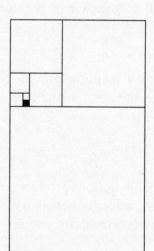

16. The perimeter of a rectangle is 38 centimeters.
The length is 7.5 centimeters. What is the width?

Additional Practice

1. **a.** Give the dimensions of the rectangle with an area of 100 square units and whole-number side lengths that has

   i. the largest perimeter

   ii. the smallest perimeter

   b. Explain how you found your answers in part (a).

2. Jim has designed a rectangle with an area of 100 square feet and a perimeter of 401 feet.

   a. Is it possible that Jim's rectangle has whole-number side lengths? Explain.

   b. What are the dimensions of Jim's rectangle?

3. Claire and Chad want to design a rectangular pen for their new puppy. They want the pen to have an area of 48 square feet. Fencing costs $0.85 per foot.

   a. What are the dimensions and the cost of the least expensive pen Claire and Chad could build, assuming the side lengths are whole numbers? Explain.

   b. What are the dimensions and the cost of the most expensive pen Claire and Chad could build, assuming the side lengths are whole numbers? Explain.

   c. Give the dimensions and the cost of a rectangular pen with whole-number side lengths and a cost between the least and most expensive pens you found in parts (a) and (b).

   d. Of the three pens you found, which one would you suggest that Claire and Chad build? Explain your choice.

Additional Practice *(continued)*

4. For each of the following, state whether the given perimeter is possible for a rectangle with an area of 42 square units and whole-number side lengths.

   a. 28 units   **b.** 46 units   **c.** 34 units   **d.** 41 units

5. On a sheet of grid paper, draw all the possible rectangles with whole-number side lengths that have a perimeter of 10 units. Explain how you made sure you did not miss any possibilities in making your rectangles.

6. For each of the following, tell whether the given area is possible for a rectangle with a perimeter of 28 units and whole-number side lengths.

   a. 24 sq. units   **b.** 40 sq. units   **c.** 42 sq. units   **d.** 45 sq. units

7. Tracy has 40 feet of material to make the perimeter of a rectangular sandbox for her little brother.

   a. What rectangle with whole-number side lengths would give the sandbox with the greatest area?

   b. What rectangle with whole-number side lengths would give the sandbox with the least area?

   c. Give the dimensions of a rectangle with whole-number side lengths that has an area between the least and greatest areas you found in parts (a) and (b).

   d. Of the three rectangles you found, which one would you recommend that Tracy make? Explain your reasoning.

Additional Practice *(continued)*

8. Travis designs a rectangle with an area of 59 square units. His rectangle is the smallest rectangle (that is, the rectangle with smallest area) with whole-number side lengths that can be made from the perimeter of the rectangle.

    a. What are the length and width of the rectangle? Explain your reasoning.

    b. What is the perimeter of the rectangle?

9. Helen designs a rectangle with an area of 225 square units. Her rectangle is the largest rectangle (that is, the rectangle with largest area) with whole-number side lengths that can be made from the perimeter of the rectangle.

    a. What are the length and width of the rectangle?

    b. What is the perimeter of the rectangle?

Skill: Changing Area, Changing Perimeter

Solve.

1. The perimeter of a rectangle is 72 m. The width of the rectangle is 16 m. What is the area of the rectangle?

2. If you have 36 ft of fencing, what are the area of the different rectangles you could enclose with the fencing? Consider only whole-number dimensions.

3. Corinda has 400 ft of fencing to make a play area. She wants the fenced area to be rectangular. What dimensions should she use in order to enclose the maximum possible area?

Additional Practice

1. Find the area and perimeter of each shape below.

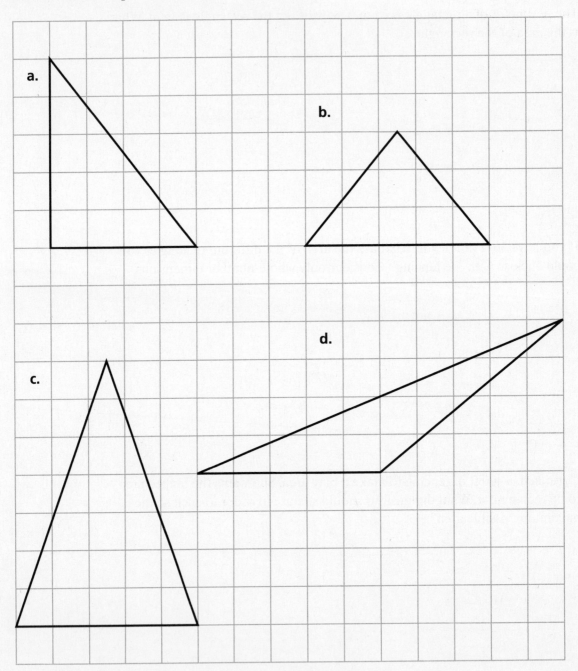

Additional Practice (continued)

2. a. Find the area of each triangle below.

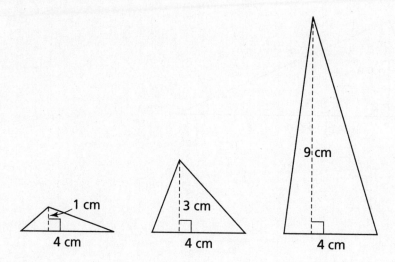

b. How are the heights of these triangles related to each other?

c. How are the areas of these triangles related to each other?

3. a. Find the area of each triangle below.

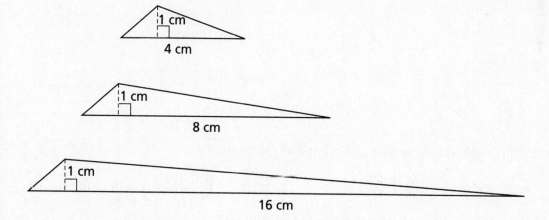

b. How are the bases of these triangles related to each other?

c. How are the areas of these triangles related to each other?

Additional Practice (continued)

4. a. Find the area of each triangle below.

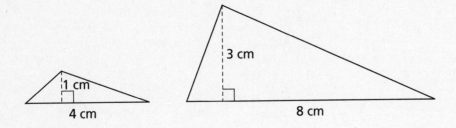

b. Based on the patterns in problems 3 and 4, sketch the third triangle.

c. How are the heights of these triangles related to each other?

d. How are the bases of these triangles related to each other?

e. How are the areas of these triangles related to each other?

Skill: Area of Triangles

Find the area of each triangle.

1.

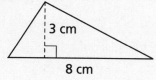

3 cm
8 cm

2.

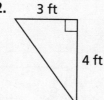

3 ft
4 ft

Tell whether each statement is *true* or *false*.

3. Two triangles that have the same base always have the same area.

4. Any obtuse triangle has a greater area than any acute triangle.

Find the area of each triangle.

5.

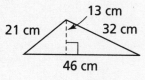

13 cm
21 cm   32 cm
46 cm

6.

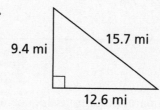

15.7 mi
9.4 mi
12.6 mi

7.

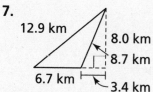

12.9 km
8.0 km
8.7 km
6.7 km
3.4 km

8.

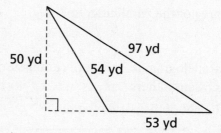

97 yd
50 yd
54 yd
53 yd

Solve.

9. The area of a triangle is 6 square units. Both the height and the length of the base are whole numbers. What are the possible lengths and heights?

Additional Practice

1. For each of the following, find the area and the perimeter of the parallelogram.

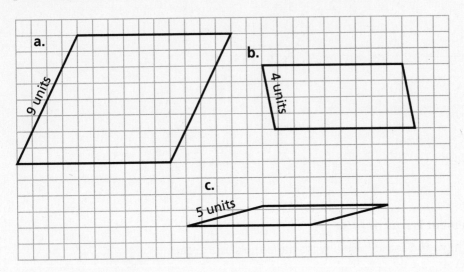

2. Use the diagram below to answer the following questions.

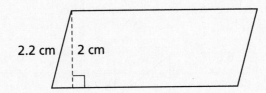

    a. If the perimeter of the parallelogram is 14.4 centimeters, what is the length of the base?

    b. What is the area of the parallelogram?

3. The area of a parallelogram is 24 square centimeters, and the base of the parallelogram is 6 centimeters.

    a. What is the height of the parallelogram?

    b. If the perimeter of the parallelogram is 22 centimeters, what is the length of the other side of the parallelogram (that is, the side that isn't the base)?

Additional Practice (continued)

4. a. Find the area of each parallelogram below.

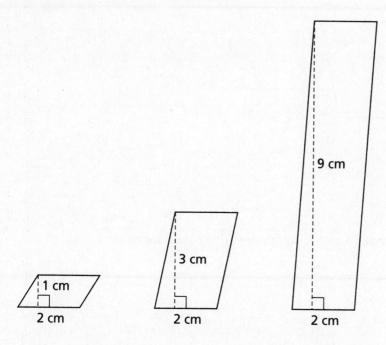

b. How are the heights of these parallelograms related to each other?

c. How are the areas of these parallelograms related to each other?

5. a. Find the area of each parallelogram below.

 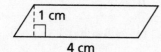 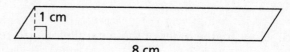

b. How are the bases of these parallelograms related to each other?

c. How are the areas of these parallelograms related to each other?

Additional Practice (continued)

6. a. Find the area of each parallelogram below.

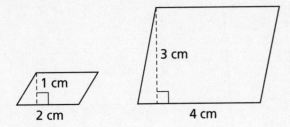

b. Based on the patterns in Exercises 4 and 5, sketch the third parallelogram.

c. How are the heights of these parallelograms related to each other?

d. How are the bases of these parallelograms related to each other?

e. How are the areas of these parallelograms related to each other?

Additional Practice (continued)

7. a. Find the area and perimeter of the triangle below.

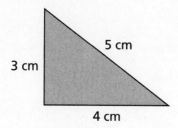

b. Find the area and perimeter of each figure below. (Figures **are** drawn to scale.)

i.

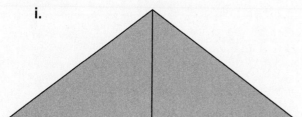

ii.

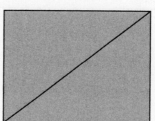

iii.

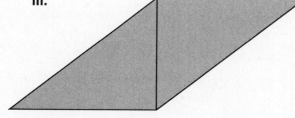

iv.

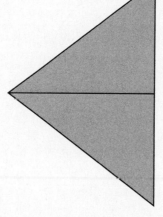

Additional Practice

Covering and Surrounding

1. For each of the following, find the circumference and the area of the circle.

a.

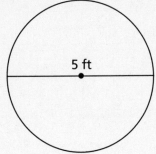

5 ft

b.

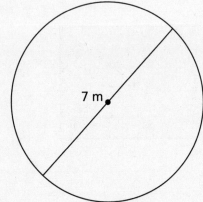

7 m

c.

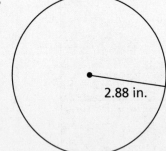

2.88 in.

Additional Practice (continued)

Covering and Surrounding

2. A circular cherry pie has a diameter of 11 inches and is cut into 8 equal-size pieces. What is the area of each piece of pie?

3. Use the diagram below to answer the following questions.

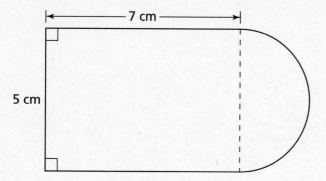

   a. What is the perimeter of the figure?

   b. What is the area of the figure?

4. Use the diagram below to answer the following questions.

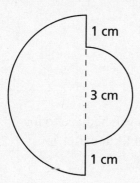

   a. What is the perimeter of the figure?

   b. What is the area of the figure?

Additional Practice (continued)

5. Below is a diagram of a jogging track. Use the diagram to answer the following questions.

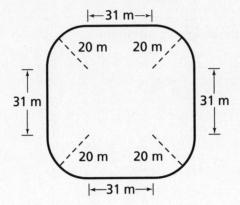

a. What is the total distance around the jogging track?

b. How much area does the jogging track enclose? Explain your reasoning.

c. Suppose Tony wants to jog 4 km. How many times will he have to jog around the track? (Remember that 1,000 meters is 1 kilometer.)

Name _____ Date _____ Class _____

Skill: Area of Circles

Investigation 5

Covering and Surrounding

Find the area of each circle. Round to the nearest tenth.

1.   3 cm

2.   2 cm

3. 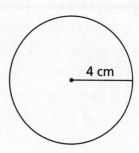 4 cm

Find the area of each circle. Round to the nearest unit. Use $\frac{22}{7}$ for π.

4. 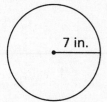 7 in.

5. 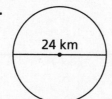 24 km

6. 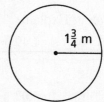 $1\frac{3}{4}$ m

Find the area of each shaded region to the nearest tenth.

7. 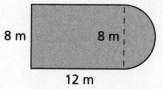 8 m 8 m 12 m

8. 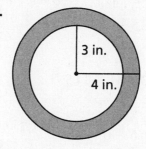 3 in. 4 in.

9. 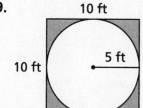 10 ft 10 ft 5 ft

79

Additional Practice

1. Rosa and Tony need to estimate how much it will cost to purchase the following supplies for their class project.

   4 pieces of posterboard at $2.89 each

   1 bottle of glue at $1.19

   2 booklets of construction paper at $4.99 each

   2 pairs of scissors at $0.59 each

   a. Estimate the cost of the supplies that Rosa and Tony need to buy. Explain.

   b. In this situation, would it be better to overestimate or underestimate? Explain.

2. Which sum is greater? Explain.

   a. 2.87 + 3.5   or   1.49 + 2.8

   b. 3.07 + 5.1   or   5.07 + 3.1

   c. 12.951 + 4.6   or   16.6 + 0.738

3. Which difference is greater? Explain.

   a. 7.3 − 4.9   or   8.5 − 3.2

   b. 25.041 − 8.3   or   31.241 − 14.5

   c. 0.57 − 0.008   or   0.6 − 0.044

4. For each list, identify the greatest value. Explain.

   a. 35.7,   35.07,   35.007

   b. 608.9,   609.8,   690.8

   c. 75.0605,   75.6050,   75.6500

Additional Practice (continued)

5. James used a calculator to complete each computation. But he forgot to write the decimal point in each answer. Write the correct answer for each computation.

Problem	Answer Without Decimal Point	Correct Answer
5.7 + 6.09 + 4.2	1599	
3.007 − 2.9 + 35.054	35161	
14.5 − 8.07 − 6.2	23	

6. Students used a computer program to test the time it took them to react to a green ball that appeared on a computer screen. Here are the reaction times for two students, a girl with initials LG and a boy with initials MC.

LG's data values:

Trial 1	Trial 2	Trial 3	Trial 4	Trial 5
1.08 sec	0.94 sec	0.64 sec	1.00 sec	0.94 sec

MC's data values:

Trial 1	Trial 2	Trial 3	Trial 4	Trial 5
1.25 sec	2.48 sec	1.15 sec	1.34 sec	1.47 sec

a. Compute the difference in LG's and MC's data values for each trial.

b. Find the sum of LG's data values.

c. Find the sum of MC's data values.

d. What are some statements you can make to compare the data from each of the two students?

7. Find the value of N that makes the number sentence true. Show your work.

a. $2.3 + 4.09 = N$ **b.** $1.009 + 12 + 0.87 = N$ **c.** $19.81 − 12.25 = N$

d. $13.7 − 10.34 = N$ **e.** $N + 3.8 = 12.65$ **f.** $N − 2.4 = 5$

Skill: Adding and Subtracting Decimals

First estimate. Then find each sum or difference.

1. $0.6 + 5.8$

2. $2.1 + 3.4$

3. $3.4 - 0.972$

4. $3.1 - 2.076$

5. $8.13 - 2.716$

6. $5.91 + 2.38$

7. $3.086 + 6.152$

8. $4.7 - 1.9$

9. $9.3 - 3.9$

10. $5.2 - 1.86$

11. $15.98 + 26.37$

12. $9.27 + 15.006$

13. $5.9 - 2.803$

14. $15.7 - 8.923$

15. $4.19 - 2.016$

16. $14.75 - 6.9264$

17. $5.1 + 4.83 + 9.002$

18. $3 + 4.02 + 8.6$

Skill: Adding and Subtracting Decimals *(continued)*

Order each set of decimals on a number line.

19. 0.2, 0.6, 0.5

20. 0.26, 0.3, 0.5, 0.59, 0.7

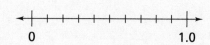

Use the table at the right for Exercise 21–23.

21. Find the sum of the decimals given in the chart. What is the meaning of this sum?

Age of Workers Earning Hourly Pay

Age of Workers	Part of Work Force
16–19	0.08
20–24	0.15
25–34	0.29
35–44	0.24
45–54	0.14
55–64	0.08
65 & over	0.02

22. What part of the hourly work force is ages 25–44?

23. Which three age groups combined represent about one-fourth of the hourly work force?

Additional Practice

1. Josh and his father are estimating how much gas they will need for a car trip. They know that the car gets 39 miles per gallon. Estimate how many gallons of gas they will need for a trip of 778 miles. Explain your reasoning.

2. The diagram below shows a rectangular plot of land cut into squares of 2.65 acres each.

    a. What is the acreage of the shaded region?

    b. What is the acreage of the unshaded region?

    c. In this area, land sells for $2,475 per acre.

        i. What would the price of the shaded region be?

        ii. What would the price of the unshaded region be?

    d. In this area, owners pay property taxes of $13.50 per thousand dollars of property value. What is the total annual property tax for the shaded and unshaded regions combined? Explain.

3. Use the number sentence $123 \times 4 = 492$ to help you solve the following:

    a. 12.3×4 **b.** 1.23×4 **c.** 0.123×4

    d. 0.123×40 **e.** 0.123×400 **f.** 0.123×4000

Additional Practice (continued)

4. Use the number sentence $63 \times 501 = 31{,}563$ to help you solve the following:

   a. 6.3×5.01 **b.** 6.3×0.501 **c.** 6.3×50.1

   d. 0.63×5.01 **e.** 0.63×501 **f.** 0.63×0.501

5. For each of the following problems, estimate the product. Explain.

   a. 2.4×0.8 **b.** 5.21×1.1

   c. 1.29×8 **d.** $12.2 \times \frac{1}{2}$

   e. 74.6×1.5 **f.** 3.04×100

6. For (a)–(f) in problem 5 above, find the product. Show your work.

7. Compute each product. What patterns do you notice?

   a. 5.5×9.9 **b.** 5.5×9.99 **c.** 5.5×9.999 **d.** 5.5×9.9999

Skill: Multiplying Decimals

Place the decimal point in each product.

1. $4.3 \times 2.9 = 1247$

2. $0.279 \times 53 = 14787$

3. $5.90 \times 6.3 = 3717$

Find each product.

4. 43.59×0.1

5. 246×0.01

6. 726×0.1

7. 5.342
    $\times\ 13$

8. 0.19
    $\times\ 0.05$

9. 6.4
    $\times\ 0.09$

10. 240
    $\times\ 0.02$

11. 43.79
    $\times\ 42$

12. 0.72
    $\times\ 0.43$

Skill: Multiplying Decimals (continued)

Use mental math to find each product.

13. 5.97×100 **14.** $4 \times 0.2 \times 5$ **15.** $3 \times (0.8 \times 1)$

16. 5.23×100 **17.** $0.38 \cdot 1{,}000$ **18.** $(5)(4.2) \times 10$

Write a number sentence you could use for each situation.

19. A pen costs \$0.59. How much would a dozen pens cost?

20. A mint costs \$0.02. How much would a roll of 10 mints cost?

21. A bottle of juice has a deposit of \$0.10 on the bottle. How much deposit money would there be on 8 bottles?

22. An orange costs \$0.09. How much would 2 dozen oranges cost?

Use $<$, $=$, or $>$ to complete each statement.

23. $2.8 \times 10 \; \blacksquare \; 26 \cdot 100$ **24.** $38.6 \cdot 10 \; \blacksquare \; 2 \cdot 38.6 \cdot 5$

25. $3.1 \times 10 \; \blacksquare \; (0.5 \cdot 0.2)3.1$ **26.** $8.3 \cdot 10 \cdot 1 \; \blacksquare \; 8.3 \times 100$

Additional Practice

1. Jason and his mother are re-tiling the kitchen floor. The area of the kitchen floor is 96.75 square feet. Each tile has an area of 1.25 square feet. How many tiles will Jason and his mother need to tile the kitchen?

2. The student concession stand buys 6.5 pounds of unpopped popcorn for $12.75. What is the price per pound of the popcorn?

3. For each of the following, decide if the quotient is less than 1 or greater than 1.
   a. $9.22 \div 2.8$ **b.** $0.9 \div 0.3$ **c.** $12.6 \div 11.8$ **d.** $5.6 \div 9.9$

4. Compute each quotient. What patterns do you notice?
   a. $6.3 \div 9$, $6.3 \div 0.9$, $6.3 \div 0.09$, $6.3 \div 0.009$

   b. $6.3 \div 9$, $0.63 \div 9$, $0.063 \div 9$, $0.0063 \div 9$

   c. $6.3 \div 9$, $0.63 \div 0.9$, $0.063 \div 0.09$, $0.0063 \div 0.009$

Additional Practice *(continued)*

5. Use the number sentence $936 \div 12 = 78$ to help you solve the following:

   a. $936 \div 1.2$ **b.** $93.6 \div 12$ **c.** $9.36 \div 12$

   d. $0.936 \div 12$ **e.** $936 \div 0.12$ **f.** $936 \div 0.012$

6. Use the number sentence $492 \div 4 = 123$ to help you solve the following:

   a. $492 \div 40$ **b.** $492 \div 400$ **c.** $492 \div 4000$

   d. $49.2 \div 4$ **e.** $4.92 \div 4$ **f.** $0.492 \div 4$

7. Find each quotient.

   a. $4.5 \div 0.3$ **b.** $64.4 \div 0.04$ **c.** $12.9 \div 20$

   d. $12.9 \div 0.2$ **e.** $1.05 \div 2.1$ **f.** $18.8 \div 4$

Skill: Dividing Decimals

Use mental math to find each quotient.

1. $7.8 \div 10$

2. $8.91 \div 100$

3. $10\overline{)46.3}$

4. $0.6 \div 10$

5. $1.45 \div 10$

6. $62.3 \div 100$

Find each quotient.

7. $0.4 \div 0.02$

8. $3.9 \div 0.05$

9. $0.2\overline{)26}$

10. $0.4\overline{)1.08}$

11. $0.68 \div 0.2$

12. $0.02\overline{)0.06}$

13. $14\overline{)889}$

14. $0.09\overline{)0.108}$

15. $0.04\overline{)0.024}$

Use $<$, $=$, or $>$ to complete each statement.

16. $56 \div 100 \ \blacksquare \ 5.6 \div 100$

17. $\$16.20 \div 10 \ \blacksquare \ \$162.00 \div 100$

Skill: Dividing Decimals (continued)

Find each quotient.

18. $1.8 \div 6$

19. $16\overline{)3.2}$

20. $17\overline{)5.1}$

21. $9\overline{)21.6}$

22. $15\overline{)123}$

23. $108 \div 5$

24. $50\overline{)17.5}$

25. $24\overline{)120.06}$

26. $9\overline{)11.24}$

Solve.

27. A package of 25 mechanical pencils costs $5.75. How much does each pencil cost?

28. A sales clerk is placing books side by side on a shelf. She has 12 copies of the same book. If the books cover 27.6 inches of the shelf, how thick is each book?

29. The salt content in the Caspian Sea is 0.13 kilograms for every liter of water. How many kilograms of salt are in 70 liters?

Find each quotient. Identify each as a terminating or repeating decimal.

30. $2.5 \div 0.08$

31. $9.6 \div 0.5$

32. $0.25 \div 0.03$

Additional Practice

1. The Oceanview Middle School sixth-grade class voted on whether to hold their class party on the second or third of April. Holding the party on April third won with 62% of the vote.

   a. What percent of the sixth-grade class voted to have the party on the second?

   b. There are 355 sixth graders at Oceanview Middle School.

   i. How many voted for having the party on the third?

   ii. How many voted for having the party on the second?

   c. The planning committee is expecting 80% of the class to attend the party. How many students are they expecting?

2. The number of registered voters in the town of Cedarville is 8,916. In the last election, Mayor Burgis won reelection with 72% of the vote.

   a. If 52% of registered voters voted in the election, how many people voted?

   b. Based on your answer to part (a), how many voters voted for Mayor Burgis?

   c. Based on your answers to parts (a) and (b), how many of those who voted did not vote for Mayor Burgis?

   d. How many registered voters would need to vote in the next election for the voter turnout to be 75%?

Additional Practice (continued)

3. Last Saturday, Aaron had lunch at a fast-food restaurant. He ordered the lunch special for $3.29. If sales tax is 6%, how much did Aaron pay for the lunch special?

4. Skateboards are on sale at Susan's Skateshop for 30% off.

   a. Express the discount as a fraction.

   b. If the regular price of a skateboard is $89, what is the discounted price?

   c. What is the total cost of the discounted skateboard in part (b) if sales tax is 4.5%?

5. The Midtown Middle School cheerleaders earned $175 at a car wash. If this amount is 25% of the cost of a new set of uniforms, what is the total cost for a set of uniforms? Explain.

6. Mary and Ms. Miller are ordering merchandise to sell in the student store. Ms. Miller says that the cost of notebooks is 125% of last year's cost.

   a. Explain what Ms. Miller means.

   b. If a notebook cost $2.00 last year, what will a notebook cost this year? Explain.

Skill: Using Percents

Solve by writing an equation.

1. Mr. Andropolis wants to leave the waitress a 12% tip. Estimate the tip he should leave if the family's bill is $32.46.

2. Michael receives a 9.8% raise. He currently earns $1,789.46 per month. Estimate the amount by which his monthly earnings will increase.

3. Estimate the sales tax and final cost of a book that costs $12.95 with a sales tax of 6%.

4. A real estate agent receives a 9% commission for every house sold. Suppose she sold a house for $112,000. Estimate her commission.

5. A jacket costs $94.95. It is on sale for 30% off. Estimate the sale price.

6. A restaurant offers a 13% discount on chicken wings on Mondays. If Travis eats $7.95 worth of chicken wings on Friday, how much would those wings cost on Monday?

7. Last year, the Widget Corporation had $650,000 in sales. This year, sales are down 4%. How much did the Widget Corporation sell this year?

8. A store is selling a sweater on sale for $17.90. The regular price is $22.95. What percent of the regular price is the sale price?

Skill: Using Percents *(continued)*

Find each amount.

9. 40% of 70

10. 25% of 80

11. 50% of 80

12. 40% of 200

13. 5% of 80

14. 75% of 200

15. 14% of 120

16. 30% of 180

17. 62.5% of 24

Solve.

18. A farmer raised a watermelon that weighed 20 lb. From his experience with raising watermelons, he estimated that 95% of the watermelon's weight is water.

   a. How much of the watermelon is water?

   b. How much of the watermelon is *not* water?

   c. The watermelon was shipped off to market. There it sat, until it had dehydrated (lost water). If the watermelon is still 90% water, what percent of it is not water?

   d. The solid part of the watermelon still weighs the same. What was the weight of the watermelon at this point?

19. A bicycle goes on sale at 75% of its original price of $160. What is its sale price?

Additional Practice

1. The student council at Metropolis Middle School conducted a survey to see whether students would prefer blue, red, or green as the new color for the school logo. The results of the survey are shown in the bar graph below.

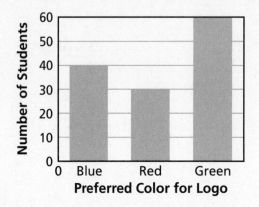

a. What is the total number of students who were surveyed?

b. What percent of students surveyed preferred blue?

c. What percent of students surveyed preferred red?

d. What percent of students surveyed preferred green?

e. If 970 students attend Metropolis Middle School, what percent of the students were surveyed?

2. What percent of 75 is 40?

3. What percent of 45 is 135? Explain your reasoning.

Additional Practice (continued)

4. 3.5 is what percent of 14?

5. What is 60% of 115?

6. What is 42.2% of 635.4?

7. Stacey's batting average on her softball team is 0.420. Becky has made 47 hits in 119 times up at bat.

   a. What percent of the time did Stacey get a hit? Show how you found your answer.

   b. What percent of the time did Becky get a hit? Show how you found your answer.

   c. During a double-header, Stacey and Becky each bat 18 times.

     i. How many hits would you expect Stacey to make?

     ii. How many hits would you expect Becky to make?

   d. Suppose Becky gets 11 hits during the double-header. Express Becky's new batting average as a decimal. Explain.

Skill: More Percents

Solve.

1. 76 is 80% of what number?

2. What is 50% of 42.88?

3. What is 85% of 120?

4. 56 is 75% of what number?

5. What percent of 80 is 50?

6. 85 is what percent of 200?

Solve.

7. The sale price of a bicycle is $120. This is 75% of the original price. Find the original price.

8. A company has 875 employees. On "Half-Price Wednesday," 64% of the employees eat lunch at the company cafeteria. How many employees eat lunch at the cafeteria on Wednesdays?

9. There are 1,295 students attending a small university. There are 714 women enrolled. What percent of the students are women?

Skill: More Percents

Solve.

10. In a recent survey, 216 people, or 54% of the sample, said they usually went to a family restaurant when they went out to eat. How many people were surveyed?

11. Juliet sold a house for $112,000. What percent commission did she receive if she earned $6,720?

12. Jason earns $200 per week plus 8% commission on his sales. How much were his sales last week if Jason earned $328?

13. Make a circle graph for the set of data.

Favorite Pet	Percent
Dogs	30%
Cats	25%
Fish	12%
Birds	11%
Other	22%

Additional Practice

1. Students at Euler Middle School are talking about ways to raise money for a school party. One student suggests a game called Heads or Tails. In this game, a player pays 50 cents and chooses heads or tails. The player then tosses a fair coin. If the coin matches the player's call, the player wins a prize.

   a. Suppose 100 players play the game. How many of these players would you expect to win?

   b. Suppose the prizes awarded to winners of the Heads or Tails game cost 40 cents each. Based on your answer to part (a), how much money would you expect the students to raise if 100 players play the game? Explain.

   c. Do you think the Heads or Tails game is an effective game for raising money for the school party? Explain your reasoning.

2. Suppose you toss a fair coin 75 times.

   a. How many times would you expect to get heads?

   b. How many times would you expect to get tails?

   c. Juan tossed a coin 75 times. The coin landed heads up 50 times and tails up 25 times. Can you conclude that the coin is not a fair coin? Explain.

Additional Practice *(continued)*

3. Joyce tossed a coin 10 times and recorded an "H" for each head and a "T" for each tail. Her results were: H, H, H, H, H, T, T, T, T, T.

   a. If you tossed a fair coin 10 times, would you expect to get the same number of heads and tails in the same order that Joyce got? Explain.

   b. Based on the results of Joyce's flips, do you think her coin is fair or not fair? Explain your reasoning.

4. Betty empties her piggy bank, which contains 210 coins, out onto her desk.

   a. How many of the coins would you expect to be heads up?

   b. How many of the coins would you expect to be tails up?

5. If you toss one coin four times in a row, which is more likely:

   a. getting 2 heads and 2 tails or getting 3 heads and 1 tail? Explain.

   b. tossing HTHT, THTH, or HHTT? Explain.

Additional Practice

1. An ordinary six-sided number cube has the numbers from 1 through 6 on its faces.

   a. If you roll a six-sided number cube, what are the possible outcomes?

   b. Suppose you roll a six-sided number cube 18 times. How many times would you expect to roll a 5? What are you assuming about the possible outcomes?

   c. Takashi and Glen are playing a game. For each turn, a number cube is rolled. If the roll is an even number, Takashi gets a point. If the roll is odd, Glen gets a point. Is this a fair game? Explain.

2. Patrick counted the cars that drove by his house over a 5-minute period. He counted a total of 27 cars.

   a. If Patrick had counted cars for an hour, about how many would you expect him to have counted?

   b. Suppose that at the same time of the day exactly one week later, Patrick counts cars over a 20-minute period. About how many cars would you expect him to count?

   c. If Patrick started counting cars after school at about 3 p.m., would you expect him to count more, fewer, or about the same number of cars than if he started counting at 5 p.m.? Explain your reasoning.

3. A bag contains 20 pieces of candy. There are 8 grape pieces, 7 cherry pieces, and 5 lemon pieces.

   a. One piece is drawn from the bag. Find the theoretical probability of drawing each flavor.

   i. P(grape)   ii. P(cherry)   iii. P(lemon)

   b. Write each of the probabilities from part (a) as a percent.

   i. P(grape)   ii. P(cherry)   iii. P(lemon)

   c. Suppose 2 grape pieces, 1 cherry piece and 1 lemon piece are removed from the bag. What is the theoretical probability of drawing each flavor now?

   i. P(grape)   ii. P(cherry)   iii. P(lemon)

   d. In part (c), what is the theoretical probability of not drawing lemon?

Additional Practice (continued)

4. A can contains eight chips. Three chips are gray, four are checkered, and one is white.

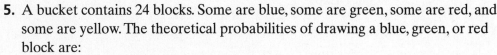

   a. What is the probability of drawing a white chip?

   b. What is the probability of drawing a checkered chip?

   c. What is the probability of drawing a gray chip?

   d. What is the probability of *not* drawing a white chip?

   e. What is the probability of *not* drawing a gray chip?

5. A bucket contains 24 blocks. Some are blue, some are green, some are red, and some are yellow. The theoretical probabilities of drawing a blue, green, or red block are:

$$P(\text{blue}) = \tfrac{1}{12}, P(\text{green}) = \tfrac{1}{8}, P(\text{red}) = \tfrac{1}{3}.$$

   a. How many blue blocks are in the bucket?

   b. How many green blocks are in the bucket?

   c. How many red blocks are in the bucket?

   d. How many yellow blocks are in the bucket?

   e. What is the probability of drawing a yellow block?

   f. What is the probability of *not* drawing a yellow block?

6. If you roll two number cubes and add the results, which is more likely, getting an even sum or getting an odd sum? Explain.

7. If you roll one number cube and add the numbers on the top and bottom faces, which is more likely, getting an even sum or getting an odd sum? Explain.

8. If you roll one number cube, is it more likely that the number rolled is a prime number or a non-prime number? Explain.

Skill: Probability

A number cube is rolled once. Find each probability.

1. $P(3)$

2. $P(\text{even})$

3. $P(1, 3, \text{or } 5)$

4. $P(0)$

5. $P(1 \text{ or } 6)$

6. $P(1 \text{ through } 6)$

A stack of 9 cards is placed face down. Each card has one letter of the word EXCELLENT. Find each probability.

7. $P(\text{E})$

8. $P(\text{N})$

9. $P(\text{T or X})$

10. $P(\text{consonant})$

There are eight blue marbles, nine orange marbles, and six yellow marbles in a bag. You draw one marble. Find each probability.

11. $P(\text{blue marble})$

12. $P(\text{yellow marble})$

13. What marble could you add or remove so that the probability of drawing a blue marble is $\frac{1}{3}$?

Skill: Probability (continued)

A box contains 12 slips of paper as shown.
Each slip of paper is equally likely to be drawn.
Find each probability.

red	blue	yellow	blue
yellow	red	blue	red
red	red	red	yellow

14. P(red)

15. P(blue)

16. P(yellow)

17. P(red) + P(blue)

18. P(red) + P(yellow)

19. P(blue) + P(yellow)

20. P(red or blue)

21. P(red or yellow)

22. P(blue or yellow)

23. P(not red)

24. P(not bluc)

25. P(not yellow)

Additional Practice

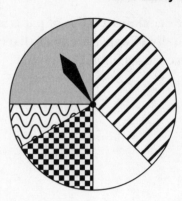

1. Use your angle ruler and the spinner at the right to answer the following questions.

   a. What fraction of the area of the spinner is gray?

   b. What fraction is checked?

   c. What fraction is marked with diagonal lines?

   d. What fraction is marked with wavy lines?

   e. What fraction is unmarked?

   f. If you were to spin the spinner 40 times, how many times would you expect it to land on the diagonally-marked region?

   g. If you were to spin the spinner 40 times, how many times would you expect it to land on the gray region?

   h. If you were to spin the spinner 40 times, how many times would you expect it to land on the unmarked region?

2. Ralph would like to make a spinner with three different colored regions so that a person would expect to spin the first color half the time, the second color one-third of the time, and the third color one-fourth of the time. Is it possible to make such a spinner? Explain.

3. Glenda has designed a spinner with blue, red, and green sections. The chances of spinning blue on Glenda's spinner are 50%, the chances of spinning red are 20%, and the chances of spinning green are 30%. Suppose you spin Glenda's spinner 50 times.

   a. How many times would you expect to spin blue?

   b. How many times would you expect to spin red?

   c. How many times would you expect to spin green?

4. Use the spinner at right to answer the following questions.

   a. What fraction of the area of the spinner is shaded gray?

   b. What fraction is unshaded?

   c. What fraction is marked with diagonal lines?

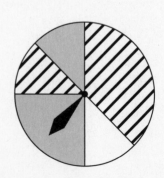

Additional Practice *(continued)*

d. Suppose you spin the spinner 72 times.

    i. How many times would you expect to spin gray?

    ii. How many times would you expect to spin the unshaded region?

    iii. How many times would you expect to spin diagonals?

5. A game called *Part or Whole?* uses the two spinners shown below.

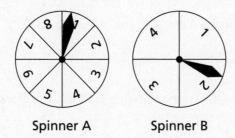

Spinner A   Spinner B

One player spins spinner A and the other spins spinner B. The number spun on spinner A is then divided by the number spun on spinner B. If the result is a fraction, the player spinning spinner A gets a point. If the quotient is a whole number, the player spinning spinner B gets a point.

a. List all the possible number pairs that can be spun with two spinners and find the quotient of each pair.

b. Is *Part or Whole?* a fair game? Explain your reasoning.

c. What is the probability of spinning a quotient of 1?

d. What is the probability of spinning a quotient of 3?

e. What is the probability of *not* spinning a quotient of $\frac{2}{3}$?

6. In which spinners below are the outcomes 1, 2, 3, and 4 equally likely? Explain.

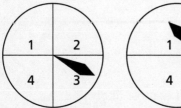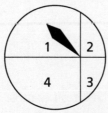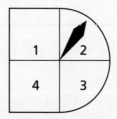

Additional Practice

1. Assuming that it is equally likely for a person to be born a boy or a girl, answer the following questions.

   a. What are all the possible outcomes (that is, each child being a boy or girl) of having two children? List the outcomes in the form (gender of first child, gender of second child).

   b. What is the probability that both children are girls?

   c. What is the probability that one child is a boy and the other is a girl?

   d. What is the probability that the oldest child is a boy?

2. Assuming that it is equally likely for a child to be born a girl or a boy, answer the following questions.

   a. Suppose a family has three children. List all the possible outcomes for the genders of the children.

   b. If a family has three children, what is the probability that all three children are girls? That all three children are boys?

   c. What is the probability of having two girls and one boy?

   d. What is the probability of having two boys and one girl?

   e. Josh has a younger brother. What is the probability that a third child will be another boy? Explain.

3. Here are two spinners. Suppose you spin both spinners.

   a. Make a chart or other diagram to show all of the outcomes.

   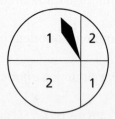 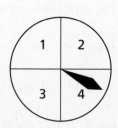

   b. Are the outcomes equally likely? If not, which ones are most likely and which ones are least likely? Explain your thinking.

Additional Practice *(continued)*

  c. Suppose you spin the spinners and add the numbers. Make a list of the possible sums.

  d. Are the sums equally likely?

4. The *Four-by-Four* game involves two four-sided number cubes with triangular faces numbered 1, 2, 3, and 4. The result of a roll is the number on the face touching the table. To play the game, players take turns rolling the cubes and adding the results. If the sum is odd, the first player gets a point. If the sum is even, the second player gets a point.

  a. List all the possible number pairs that can be rolled and the sum for each pair.

  b. Is *Four-by-Four* a fair game? Explain your reasoning.

  c. Which sum is most likely, and what is its probability?

  d. What is the probability of rolling a sum of 6?

  e. What is the probability of rolling a sum of 3?

  f. What is the probability of *not* rolling a sum of 8? Explain.

5. Suppose the rules of *Four-by-Four* are kept the same except that instead of finding the sum of the two numbers rolled, you find the product.

  a. List all the possible products that can be rolled.

  b. Is this version of *Four-by-Four* a fair game? Explain your reasoning.

  c. Which product is most likely, and what is its probability?

  d. What is the probability of rolling a product of 5?

  e. What is the probability of rolling a product of 12?

  f. What is the probability of *not* rolling a product of 2?

  g. What is the probability of rolling a product greater than 3?

Additional Practice (continued)

6. A game is played by rolling a four-sided number cube with faces numbered 1, 2, 3, 4 and a six-sided number cube with faces numbered 1, 2, 3, 4, 5, 6 and finding the sum of the numbers rolled.

   A player wins by rolling a sum of 2, 3, 4, 9, or 10; otherwise, the player loses.

   a. List all the possible number pairs that can be rolled and find the sum of each pair.

   b. Is this game fair or unfair? Explain your reasoning.

   c. What is the probability of rolling a sum of 7?

   d. What is the probability of rolling a sum of 4?

   e. What is the probability of rolling a sum of 9?

   f. If you played this game 48 times, how many times would you expect to win? How many times would you expect to lose?

   g. Suppose the game costs 25 cents to play, and if you win you get 50 cents. Suppose you play the game 48 times. Use your answers from part f to answer the following questions:

      i. How much money would it cost to play 48 times?

      ii. How much money would you expect to win?

      iii. How much would you expect to win or lose all together after playing the game 48 times?

Skill: Experimental and Theoretical Probability

Each shape in a set of blocks comes in two sizes (small and large), three colors (yellow, red, and blue), and two thicknesses (thick and thin).

   1. Draw a tree diagram to find the total number of outcomes.

   2. How many outcomes are possible?   3. How many outcomes will be red?

   4. How many outcomes will be blue and thin?   5. How many outcomes will be large?

   6. Suppose a medium size is also available. How many outcomes are possible now?

A box contains ten balls, numbered 1 through 10. Marisha draws a ball. She records its number and then returns it to the bag. Then Penney draws a ball. Find each probability.

   7. P(9, then 3)   8. P(even, then odd)

   9. P(odd, then 2)   10. P(the sum of the numbers is 25)

   11. P(prime, then composite)   12. P(a factor of 8, then a multiple of 2)

Additional Practice

1. Ms. Snow's students wrote down a whole number between 1 and 10 on a slip of paper. She collected the numbers and displayed the data in the line plot below.

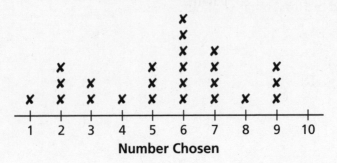

Number Chosen

   a. What is the typical number chosen by students in this class?

   b. If two students were absent on the day Ms. Snow collected the data, how many students are enrolled in the class? Explain your reasoning.

2. Mr. Watkins arranged the quiz scores of his afternoon math class from least to greatest: 5, 5, 6, 6, 6, 7, 7, 7, 7, 7, 8, 8, 8, 8, 8, 8, 9, 9, 9, 10, 10

   a. How many students are in Mr. Watkins's afternoon math class?

   b. How do the quiz scores vary?

   c. What is the mode of the scores?

   d. What is the median of the scores?

3. The students in Mr. Furgione's math class counted the letters in the names of the streets where they lived. Then they made the bar graph below.

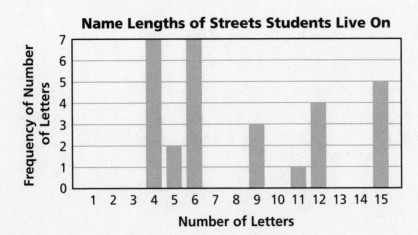

Name Lengths of Streets Students Live On

Additional Practice (continued)

a. Use the bar graph on page 116 to make a table showing each name length and the number of students who live on streets with names of that length. Then make a line plot showing these name lengths.

b. Nobody was absent when the data were collected. How many students are in Mr. Furgione's class? Explain your reasoning.

c. What is the typical street-name length for this class? Use the mode, median, and range to help you answer this question.

For Exercises 4–7, make a line plot or a bar graph of a set of name-length data that fits the description.

4. 24 names that vary from 6 letters to 18 letters

5. 9 names with a median of 12 letters

Additional Practice *(continued)*

6. 11 names that vary from 6 to 15 letters and a median of 13 letters

7. 14 names with a median of 12 letters and a range of 7 letters to 17 letters

8. Mr. Wanko's classroom looks out over one of the school's parking lots. His class made the bar graph at right of the colors of the vehicles parked in the lot.

a. Does the bar graph show categorical or numerical data? Explain.

b. How many vehicles are parked in the lot?

c. Which vehicle color seems most popular? Explain.

d. Suppose Mr. Wanko's class collected data on the colors of vehicles parked in the same lot next week and represented the data in a bar graph. Would you expect this new bar graph to be the same as the one above? Why or why not?

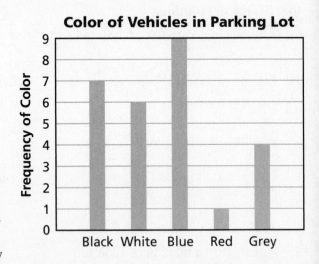

Color of Vehicles in Parking Lot

9. Edna rolled a pair of six-sided number cubes several times and recorded the sums on the line plot at right.

a. Which roll(s) occurred most often? Explain your reasoning.

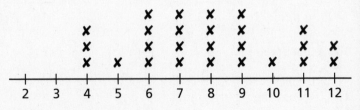

Additional Practice (continued)

b. How many times did Edna roll the cubes? Explain how you found your answer.

c. How do the sums on Edna's line plot vary?

d. What is the median sum? Explain.

e. Does Edna's line plot show categorical or numerical data? Explain.

f. Suppose you roll a pair of number cubes the same number of times as Edna did. Would you expect a line plot of your results to look exactly like Edna's? Explain.

Tell whether the answers to the question are numerical or categorical data.

10. What is your foot length in centimeters?

11. How many hand spans are needed to measure the length of your desk?

12. What is your favorite movie?

13. On a scale of 1 to 5, with 1 being poor and 5 being excellent, rate how you felt in your last gym class.

14. Are more students born in January or in August?

15. What is the typical amount of sleep students in your class had last night?

Use this line plot for questions 16 and 17 below.

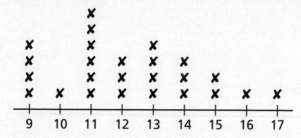

Name Lengths of Mr. Samuel's Students

16. What is the median name length for this class?

   A. 13   **B.** 12   **C.** 11   **D.** 3

17. How do the name lengths for this class vary?

   F. 1 to 6   **G.** 9 to 17   **H.** 4 to 1   **J.** none of these

Skill: Line Plots

Ms. Makita made a line plot to show the scores her students got on a test. At the right is Ms. Makita's line plot.

1. What does each data item or ✗ represent?

2. How many more students scored 75 than scored 95?

3. How many students scored over 85?

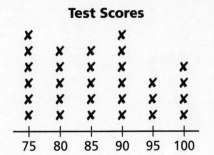

Test Scores

4. What scores did the same number of students get?

For Exercises 5–8, use the line plot at the right.

5. What information is displayed in the line plot?

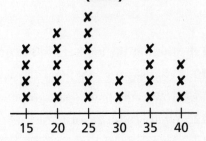

Time Spent Doing Homework Last Night (min)

6. How many students spent time doing homework last night?

7. How many students spent at least half an hour on homework?

8. How did the time spent on homework last night vary?

9. A kennel is boarding dogs that weigh the following amounts (in pounds).

| 5 | 62 | 43 | 48 | 12 | 17 | 29 | 74 |
| 8 | 15 | 4 | 11 | 15 | 26 | 63 | |

   a. How do the dogs' weights vary?

   b. How many of the dogs weigh under 50 pounds?

116

Additional Practice

1. The members of the drama club sold candy bars to help raise money for the school's next play. The stem-and-leaf plot below shows how many candy bars each member of the drama club sold.

Candy Bars Sold by Drama Club

```
1 | 0 1 1 1 2 3 5 6 9
2 | 1 1 1 1 4 7
3 | 2 3 4 8
4 | 1 4 9
5 | 2 3 5 5 8
```

Key: 3 | 2 means 32 candy bars

   a. How many students are in the drama club?

   b. How many students sold 25 or more candy bars?

   c. How do the numbers of candy bars sold by each student vary?

   d. What is the typical number of candy bars sold by each student?

2. Earl rolls 6 six-sided number cubes and finds the sum of the numbers rolled.

   a. What are the least and greatest sums Earl can roll? Explain.

   b. What do your answers for part (a) tell you about the sums Earl can roll?

   c. Earl rolled the number cubes several times and recorded each sum. Here are Earl's results:

   27, 21, 17, 18, 21, 18, 25, 32, 8, 19, 21, 20, 26, 21, 11, 23, 33, 19, 9, 12, 17

   Make a stem-and-leaf plot to display Earl's data.

   d. Using your stem plot, find the typical sum rolled. Use the median and range to explain your reasoning.

Additional Practice (continued)

3. Taryn and Travis work in the student store at their school. They made the coordinate graph below to show the total sales each day for three weeks. There are three points corresponding to each weekday because Taryn and Travis recorded their data for the three weeks on a one-week graph.

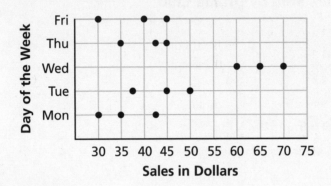

a. What were the total sales on Tuesdays for the three weeks Taryn and Travis collected their data?

b. Which day of the week seems to be the best for sales at the student store? Explain your reasoning.

c. Which day of the week varies the most for total sales? Explain.

d. How do the sales for the entire three-week period vary?

e. What is the median of the total sales for Fridays? What is the median of the total sales for the three weeks Taryn and Travis collected data?

f. Describe the pattern of sales during a typical week at the student store.

Name _____ Date _____ Class _____

Additional Practice (continued)

4. Emily rolled two four-sided number cubes 12 times and computed the sum for each roll. She recorded the results as ordered pairs. The first coordinate is the number of the roll, and the second coordinate is the sum for that roll. For example, $(9, 2)$ means that on her ninth roll Emily rolled a sum of two. The results of Emily's rolls were: $(1, 7), (2, 8), (3, 3), (4, 4), (5, 6), (6, 3), (7, 5), (8, 6),$ $(9, 2), (10, 4), (11, 5), (12, 5).$

   a. Make a coordinate graph of Emily's data. Use the horizontal axis for the number of the roll and the vertical axis for the result.

   b. What is the mode of the sums of Emily's rolls? Explain.

   c. How do the sums vary?

   d. What is the median of the sums? Explain.

   e. Does the coordinate graph you made in part (a) show a pattern in Emily's number-cube rolls? Explain.

For Exercises 5–7, use the stem-and-leaf plot below.

Students' Foot Lengths

```
1 | 7
2 | 0 0 0 0 1 1 1 1 2 2 2 2 2 2 2 3 3 4 4 4 5 5 6 7 7 8
3 | 0 2
```

5. How many students are in the class?
   A. 3   **B.** 12   **C.** 30   **D.** 33

6. How do the foot lengths for this class vary?
   F. 1 to 3   **G.** 7 to 2   **H.** 17 to 32   **J.** 20 to 28

7. What is the median foot length for this class?
   A. 2   **B.** 20   **C.** 22   **D.** 24.5

Name _____ Date _____ Class _____

Skill: Stem-and-Leaf Plots

The stem-and-leaf plot at the right shows the number of baskets scored by one of ten intramural teams last season.

5	2 6 9
6	0 4 6
7	1 5
8	4 8

Key: 8 | 4 means 84

1. How many data items are there?

2. What is the least measurement given?

3. What is the greatest measurement given?

4. In how many games did the team score less than 70 baskets?

For Exercises 5–11, use the stem-and-leaf plot below.

5. What is the age of the youngest grandparent?

Ages of Grandparents

stem	leaf
6	7 8 8
7	0 1 2 3 4 9 9
8	1 3 3 3 4 7
9	0 2 5

Key: 7 | 0 means 70

6. What is the age of the oldest grandparent?

7. How many grandparents are 79 years old?

8. How many grandparents are older than 74?

9. How does the data vary?

10. What is the median?

11. What is the mode?

Additional Practice

1. The mean amount of change that Betty, Bill, and Susan have in their pockets is 79 cents. What is the total value of the change they have together? Explain.

2. Glenda rolled two six-sided number cubes nine times and computed the sum of the numbers rolled each time.

   a. If the mean sum of Glenda's rolls was 6, what was the total of the nine sums Glenda rolled?

   b. Suppose Glenda's rolls were 12, 7, 3, 10, 9, 2, 11, 7, and 8.
      i. What is the median of Glenda rolls?

      ii. What is the mean of Glenda's rolls?

      iii. What is the mode of Glenda's rolls?

      iv. Which do you think is the best indicator of a typical roll Glenda made, the median, mean, or mode? Explain your reasoning.

   c. Suppose Glenda rolled a total sum of 60 for her nine rolls.
      i. What is the mean sum for the rolls Glenda made?

      ii. Give an example of nine rolls that Glenda could have made. Explain.

3. Mrs. Wilcox asked each of her students to spin a spinner with 50 equal sections labeled with whole numbers between 1 and 50. Below is a stem-and-leaf plot showing the results of the students' spins.

   a. How many students arc in Mrs. Wilcox's class?

   b. What is the median number of spins by Mrs. Wilcox's students?

   c. What is the mean number of spins by Mrs. Wilcox's students?

0	3 3 6 6
1	0 1 2 3 4 9 9
2	0 0 1 2 2 4 5 6
3	4 8 9
4	1 1 2 3 9
5	0

   Key: 2 | 4 means 24

   d. Which is the better measure of a typical number of spins by a student in Mrs. Wilcox's class, the median or the mean? Explain your reasoning.

Additional Practice (continued)

4. The students in North Middle School had a contest to see who could save the most money. The mean savings in Ms. Jones' class (25 students) was the same as the mean savings for the whole school (300 students). The mean amount was $16.00.

   a. What is the total savings for Ms. Jones' students? Explain.

   b. What is the total savings for the whole school? Explain.

5. Every student in Mr. Smith's class tossed 3 coins and counted the number of heads. The bar graph below displays their results.

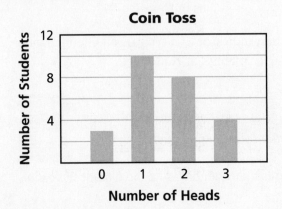

   a. How many students are in Mr. Smith's class?

   b. What is the mean number of heads?

   c. What is the median number of heads?

   d. How many heads did the students toss altogether?

   e. How many tails did the students toss altogether?

Additional Practice (continued)

6. The Cycle Shoppe sells 10 brands of bicycles with these prices:

    $90, $130, $180, $280, $320, $390, $670, $840, $1050, $1400

    a. What is the mean price?

    b. What is the median price?

    c. Which price seems most typical? Explain your reasoning.

For Exercises 7 and 8, use this information.
    Mr. Johnson's class of 20 students collects 180 cans of food for the food drive.
    Ms. Smith's class of 25 students collects 200 cans of food.

7. Which class has a greater mean number of cans of food?

    A. Mr. Johnson's class

    B. Ms. Smith's class

    C. The means are equal.

    D. There isn't enough information to tell.

8. Which class has a greater median number of cans of food?

    F. Mr. Johnson's class

    G. Ms. Smith's class

    H. The means are equal.

    J. There isn't enough information to tell.

Skill: Mean, Median, and Mode

For Exercises 1–3, use the table.

1. What is the mean height of the active volcanoes listed to the nearest foot?

2. What is the median height of the active volcanoes listed?

3. What is the mode of the heights of the active volcanoes listed?

Active Volcanoes	
Name	**Height Above Sea Level (ft)**
Cameroon Mt.	13,354
Mount Erebus	12,450
Asama	8,300
Gerde	9,705
Sarychev	5,115
Ometepe	5,106
Fogo	9,300
Mt. Hood	11,245
Lascar	19,652

The sum of the heights of all the students in a class is 1,472 in.

4. The mean height is 5 ft 4 in. How many students are in the class? (1 ft = 12 in.)

5. The median height is 5 ft 2 in. How many students are 5 ft 2 in. or taller? How many are shorter?

The number of pages read (to the nearest multiple of 50) by the students in history class last week are shown in the tally table.

Pages	50	100	150	200	250	300	350	400	450	500	550	600	650	700	750
Tally	I		II	┼┼┼ I	I	┼┼┼	III	IIII	I	I					I

6. Find the mean, the median, and the mode of the data.

7. Are there any outliers in this set of data.

8. Do any outliers raise or lower the mean?

9. Would you use the mean, median, or mode to most accurately reflect the typical number of pages read by a student? Explain.